Book 2

Maths Games

Number Games

Caroline Clissold
Sue Atkinson

HOPSCOTCH
LIONAL SHING

CONTENTS

Published by
Hopscotch Educational Publishing Ltd.,
Unit 2, The Old Brushworks, 56 Pickwick Road,
Corsham, Wiltshire SN13 9BX
Tel: 01249 701701

© 2003 Hopscotch Educational Publishing

Written by Caroline Clissold
Series consultant: Sue Atkinson
Series design by Blade Communications
Illustrated by Susan Hutchison
Printed by Clintplan Limited, Southam

ISBN 1-904307-45-0

Caroline Clissold and Sue Atkinson hereby assert
their moral right to be identified as the author of this
work in accordance with the Copyright, Designs and
Patents Act, 1988.

The author would like to thank the many
teachers and children from the following
schools who trialled these activities:

Bishop Perrin Primary School,
Richmond

Sheen Mount Primary School,
Richmond

Upton House School, Windsor

Kinsale Middle School, Hellesdon,
Norwich

Eye Primary School, Peterborough

Happisburgh First School, Norfolk

Aslacton Primary School, Norfolk

Alpington Primary School, Norfolk

Scarning Primary School, Dereham,
Norfolk

West Thurrock Primary School, Essex

St Josephs Primary School, Stanford-le-
Hope, Essex

Playing maths games has been shown to have a positive influence on children's learning. This series of books is designed to raise achievement in your class.

This book of games is suitable for children who are:
- working on learning objectives from about levels 2 or 3 to games suitable for Years 7, 8 and 9 average and high achievers. (For the lower achievers you might need to work from *Book 1* which has artwork designed to be suitable for all ages.);
- lower achievers in Key Stage 3. (The artwork has been designed to be suitable for use with older children.);
- in need of more practice with certain key objectives in the National Numeracy Framework.

Using the games

The games are clearly differentiated and are suitable for:
- the whole class to play at the same time;
- working independently in group-work time;
- working with other adults in the classroom;
- use at home as homework or borrowed as part of a maths games library.

It is important to refer to the objectives for the other year groups to give your groups/class a range of differentiated games.

The structure of the book

The chart/contents list on page 5 shows the main learning objective for each of the games.

Each game has a double page of teacher's notes followed by photocopiable game boards and/or cards specific to that game. Any resource that is needed for more than one of the games is called a generic sheet; these are at the back of the book.

Also at the back of the book are the rules of the games, presented in such a way that they can be cut out, mounted onto card and used by the children. See page 4 for more information on the rules.

The structure of the teacher's notes

These show the main learning objective, the resources required, how to play the game, variations for the different age ranges and ideas for the plenary session.

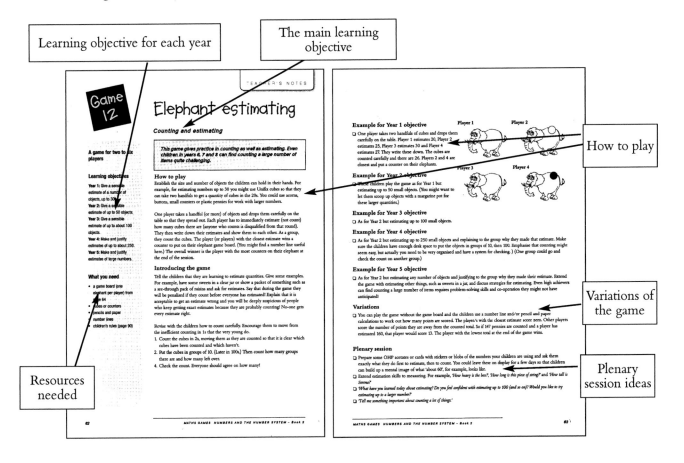

Preparing the games

The teacher's notes will tell you what you need to play the games and which pages you need to photocopy. You can copy the game boards onto card if you want, or onto paper and laminate them.

The photocopiable number cards, spinners and counters are best copied onto card before they are cut for ease of handling them.

Using the spinners

When you cut out each spinner, cut out the rectangle of card that it is drawn on because having this to hold makes spinning the paper-clip easier.

With one hand, trap the paper-clip with the pencil in the middle of the spinner. Flick the paper-clip around with a finger on the other hand. If the clip stops on a line, that player can decide which of the two sections he or she wants.

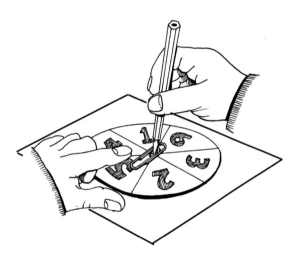

Rules for the games

Rules for the games are explained in the teacher's notes. At the back of the book the rules are presented in such a way that they can be cut out, mounted onto card and used by the children. Some of the games have two versions of the rules. Some of the rules contain blank boxes for the teacher to complete with the relevant numbers to be used in the game. There is a blank rules card which can be used for variations of the games. You might find it helpful for a games library always to stick a copy of the rules on the back of each game, as well as a copy of the rules that can be referred to as the game is played.

Storing the games

Store the games in plastic folders that have been labelled to show the title of the game, the learning objective and the contents of the folder (for example '1 game board, 2 spinners, rules, 4 counters').

A final note

Above all, boost children's self-esteem by your focussed assessment questions and your praise and encouragement, so that maths is enjoyed by everyone.

Linking maths concepts to the games in this book

	Game 1	Game 2	Game 3	Game 4	Game 5	Game 6	Game 7	Game 8	Game 9	Game 10	Game 11	Game 12	Game 13	Game 14
Count on or back in different steps from different numbers	✓	✓	✓											
Know what each digit represents in different numbers		✓	✓	✓	✓	✓					✓	✓		
Partitioning numbers			✓	✓	✓	✓								
Understand and use decimal notation and place value	✓	✓	✓	✓	✓	✓								
Comparing and ordering numbers					✓	✓					✓			
Rounding									✓	✓			✓	
Estimating and approximating												✓	✓	
Recognising odd and even numbers							✓	✓						✓
Making general statements							✓	✓						✓
Assessment														✓

Game
1

Big foot

Counting in different steps

This game can be adapted to counting in steps of any size.

A game for two to four players

Learning objectives

Year 2: Count on or back in 10s and 2s, starting from any two-digit number.

Year 3: Count on or back in 2s, 10s or 100s, starting from any two-digit number.

Year 4: Count on in steps of 25 to 500 and back to, say, 100.

Year 5: Count on in steps of 25 to 1,000, and then back; Count on or back in steps of 0.1, 0.2, 0.3.

Years 6 & 7: Count on in steps of 0.1, 0.2, 0.25, 0.5, and then back.

What you need

- number line game boards, one for each child, with the number at the end of the line filled in appropriately (page 8)
- instruction cards (pages 9–14)
- a pile of cubes or foot counters (page 15) for each child
- children's rules (page 80)
- number lines

How to play

Each player has at least one number line. Place a pile of instruction cards face down in the middle of the table (choose from pages 9 to 14 according to the needs of your class). Players take it in turns to pick a card. If the card tells them to count on, they should count on from the 0 at the beginning of their number line the number of steps instructed and place their foot counter or a cube on the last step. They then write their number below that mark. If they pick a card that tells them to count back, they should start at the other end of the line. If anyone lands on a point on their board that is already covered, they cannot place a counter and play passes to the next player.

Introducing the game

Say to the children *'You are going to play a game that will help you to learn to count on in steps of different numbers.'* Explain that the aim is to place a foot counter on every point on a number line in response to instructions to count on or back.

Example for Year 3 objective

❑ Players have two number lines, one marked in 10s from 0 to 100 (so write 100 at the end of the line) and the other marked from 0 to 20 in 2s (so write 20 at the end of the line). They also need the cards from pages 9 and 10.

❑ Player 1 picks up a card that reads 'Count on in 2s to 18'. They need the number line that ends in 20. They should use the foot counter to count along the line in 2s to 18, with each point on the number line representing a step of 2. They then put their foot counter on the mark for 18 and write 18 underneath.

❑ Player 2 picks a card that reads 'Count back in 10s to 30', so they need the number line that ends in 100. They counts back from 100 and place their counter on the 30.

❑ The first player to complete both of their lines is the winner.

❑ (Once the children are confident, let them play the game using the counting in 5s cards on page 11 as well. They will need three number lines for this.)

MATHS GAMES **NUMBERS AND THE NUMBER SYSTEM – Book 2**

Example for Year 2 objective

❏ Use the same basic rules as for the Year 3 example but with a number line marked from 0 to 100 and the cards on page 9 only. Play with cards for counting in 2s in a separate game until the children are confident. Then, when they are confident, you could use the counting in 5s cards on page 11.

Example for Year 4 objective

❏ These children can use three number lines. The third one ends in 250. Include the cards for counting in 25s (page 12) as well as 10s and 2s.

Example for Year 5 objective

❏ Each player needs three number lines. Choose three sets of cards to use, for example 0.1s, 25s and use the blank set for counting in 0.2s. Remember to put the end number on each line, or agree that with the children.

Example for Years 6 and 7 objective

❏ These children play the game as for Year 5, using the 'blank' cards on page 14 for 3 sets of numbers suitable for this group, for example counting in steps of 0.3 or 100s. Alternatively give groups a copy of the blank cards and ask them to make up a game to challenge another group. They must write three ending numbers on the sheet of number lines.

❏ Make cards for counting in 0.25s and 0.5s.

❏ You could use the blank cards to make cards for measuring, for example to count in steps of 1mm to 1cm or 2m.

❏ Another game is to position zero on a number line so that negative numbers are used.

Variations

❏ Use different numbers to start the number line. For example, you could start from 50, 100, 125, 1000, 2.5 and so on.

❏ Adapt the game for counting in 3s, 4s, 6s and so on, when learning multiplication tables, using the blank rules on page 88 filled in by you or the children.

Plenary session

❏ Invite some of the children who have played the game to explain to the others what they have been doing and what it has helped them to practise.

❏ Have a bag of number cards with the appropriate numbers on them for the group. Invite some children out to the front of the class to take a card out of the bag. Whichever card they pick they should count on in the steps you tell them. For example, for Year 5, one child might pick out a card that has 0.3 on it. Ask them to count on in steps of 0.3.

❏ When a few children have had a turn, ask *What did you learn today?*

❏ *If I was counting in 2s and I had to count from zero to 16, how many hops along the number line would I have to do?*

❏ *If I was counting in 0.25s and I marked one whole one, how many steps did I take? What is a quarter of one whole one? Show how you work that out on your number line.*

Number lines

Name: _____

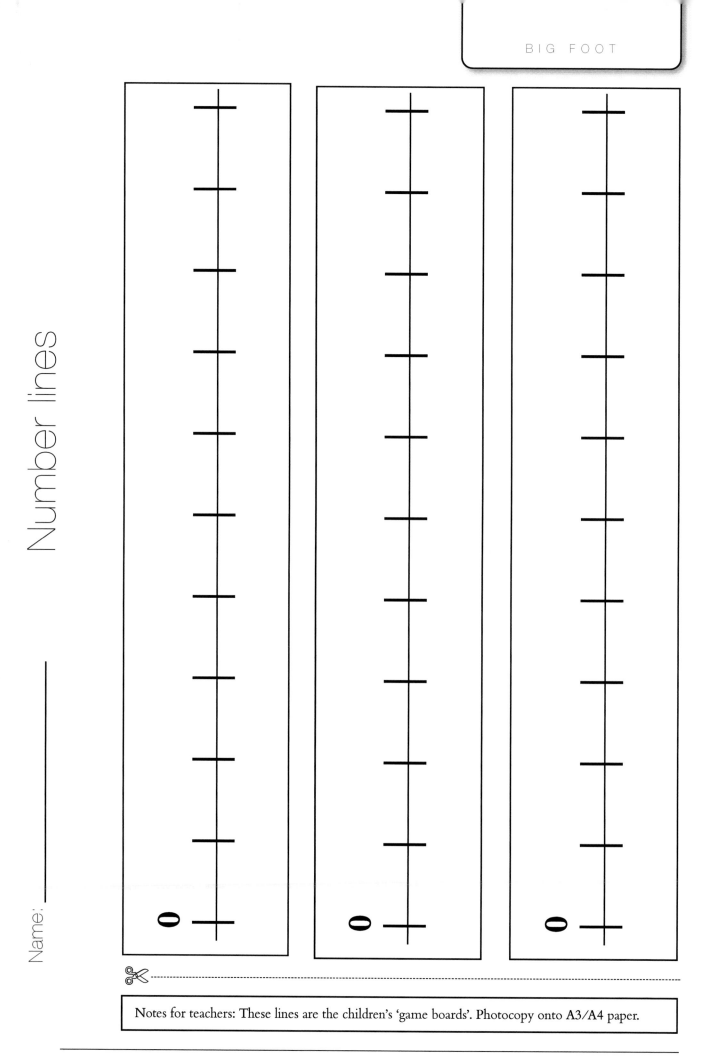

Notes for teachers: These lines are the children's 'game boards'. Photocopy onto A3/A4 paper.

Cards for counting in 10s

Count on in 10s to 10	Count on in 10s to 20	Count on in 10s to 30	Count on in 10s to 40	Count on in 10s to 50
Count on in 10s to 60	Count on in 10s to 70	Count on in 10s to 80	Count on in 10s to 90	Count on in 10s to 100
Count back in 10s to 10	Count back in 10s to 20	Count back in 10s to 30	Count back in 10s to 40	Count back in 10s to 0
Count back in 10s to 60	Count back in 10s to 70	Count back in 10s to 80	Count back in 10s to 90	Count back in 10s to 50

Notes for teachers: Photocopy these cards onto A3 paper and cut out. Use them with a zero to 100 number line.

Cards for counting in 2s

Count on in 2s to 10	Count on in 2s to 8	Count on in 2s to 6	Count on in 2s to 4
Count on in 2s to 20	Count on in 2s to 18	Count on in 2s to 16	Count on in 2s to 14
Count back in 2s to 8	Count back in 2s to 6	Count back in 2s to 4	Count back in 2s to 2
Count back in 2s to 18	Count back in 2s to 16	Count back in 2s to 14	Count back in 2s to 12
		Count back in 2s to 0	Count back in 2s to 10

Count on in 2s to 2

Count on in 2s to 12

Notes for teachers: Photocopy these cards onto A3 paper and cut out. Use them with a zero to 20 number line.

Cards for counting in 5s

Count on in 5s to 5	Count on in 5s to 10	Count on in 5s to 15	Count on in 5s to 20	Count on in 5s to 25
Count on in 5s to 30	Count on in 5s to 35	Count on in 5s to 40	Count on in 5s to 45	Count on in 5s to 50
Count back in 5s to 0	Count back in 5s to 5	Count back in 5s to 10	Count back in 5s to 15	Count back in 5s to 20
Count back in 5s to 25	Count back in 5s to 30	Count back in 5s to 35	Count back in 5s to 40	Count back in 5s to 45

✂ --

Notes for teachers: Photocopy these cards onto A3 paper and cut out. Use them with a zero to 50 number line.

Cards for counting in 25s

Count on in 25s to 25	Count on in 25s to 50	Count on in 25s to 75	Count on in 25s to 100	Count on in 25s to 125
Count on in 25s to 150	Count on in 25s to 175	Count on in 25s to 200	Count on in 25s to 225	Count on in 25s to 250
Count back in 25s to 0	Count back in 25s to 25	Count back in 25s to 50	Count back in 25s to 75	Count back in 25s to 100
Count back in 25s to 125	Count back in 25s to 150	Count back in 25s to 175	Count back in 25s to 200	Count back in 25s to 225

Notes for teachers: Photocopy these cards onto A3 paper and cut out. Use them with a zero to 250 number line.

Cards for counting in 0.1s

Count on in 0.1s to 0.1	Count on in 0.1s to 0.2	Count on in 0.1s to 0.3	Count on in 0.1s to 0.5
Count on in 0.1s to 0.6	Count on in 0.1s to 0.7	Count on in 0.1s to 0.8	Count on in 0.1s to 0.10
Count back in 0.1s to 0	Count back in 0.1s to 0.1	Count back in 0.1s to 0.2	Count back in 0.1s to 0.4
Count back in 0.1s to 0.5	Count back in 0.1s to 0.6	Count back in 0.1s to 0.7	Count back in 0.1s to 0.9

Count on in 0.1s to 0.4

Count on in 0.1s to 0.9

Count back in 0.1s to 0.3

Count back in 0.1s to 0.8

Notes for teachers: Photocopy these cards onto A3 paper and cut out. Use them with a zero to 1 number line.

Blank cards for use in any game

Count on in ☐ s one point along your line.	Count on in ☐ s two points along your line.	Count on in ☐ s three points along your line.	Count on in ☐ s four points along your line.	Count on in ☐ s five points along your line.
Count on in ☐ s six points along your line.	Count on in ☐ s seven points along your line.	Count on in ☐ s eight points along your line.	Count on in ☐ s nine points along your line.	Count on in ☐ s ten points along your line.
Count back in ☐ s one point along your line.	Count back in ☐ s two points along your line.	Count back in ☐ s three points along your line.	Count back in ☐ s four points along your line.	Count back in ☐ s five points along your line.
Count back in ☐ s six points along your line.	Count back in ☐ s seven points along your line.	Count back in ☐ s eight points along your line.	Count back in ☐ s nine points along your line.	Count back in ☐ s ten points along your line.

Notes for teachers: Game cards for you to fill in for use with other numbers. Remember to number the right end of the number line appropriately.

'Big foot' counters

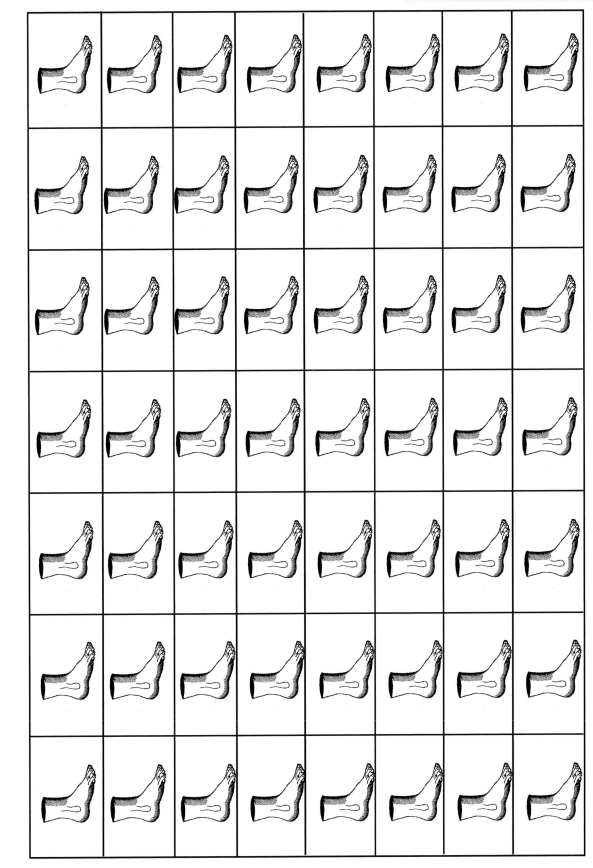

✂ -

Notes for teachers: Photocopy and cut out.

Game 2

Count it!

Counting in steps and addition of money

This game can be adapted for any numbers, so you can differentiate for all your groups. The addition of money also needs to be differentiated.

A game for two players

Year 2: Count on or back in 1s or 10s, starting from any two-digit number.

Year 3: Count on or back in 5s, 10s or 100s, starting from any two- or three-digit number.

Year 4: Count on in steps of 25 to 500 and back.

Year 5: Count on in steps of 25 to 1,000 and then back; count on or back in steps of 0.1, 0.2, 0.3.

Year 6: Count on in steps of 0.1, 0.2, 0.25, 0.5 and then back.

Years 7 & 8: Count on and back in decimal steps including hundredths.

What you need

- a game board photocopied onto A3 paper (pages 18 to 20)
- game cards (enlarged) placed in a pack on the table beside the game board (pages 21 to 23)
- counters, one different colour for each player
- a pot of money
- children's rules (page 80)

How to play

Players place their counters on 'Start'. They take it in turns to pick a 'Count it' card from the pack. Each player follows the instructions on their card. So, if the card says 'Start counting at 0 and count on in 5s to 25', that player counts '5, 10, 15, 20, 25', moving their counter on one space around the board as they say each one. In this case they move five spaces, counting in a clockwise direction. If the card says 'Start at 40 and count back in 10s to 20', the child moves in an anti-clockwise direction two spaces, counting '30, 20'. They leave their counter where they land. If a player lands on a 'collect' rectangle, they collect and save that amount of money. Play continues in this manner until the end of the session or when a time limit given by the teacher is up. The winner is the player with the most money.

Introducing the game

Tell the children that they are learning to count on or back in steps of different numbers and that this game will help to reinforce that.

Example for Year 2 objective

- ❏ Prepare cards to suit your children from the Cards 1 sheet. They are used on Game board 1.
- ❏ Player 1 picks a card that says 'Start at 20 and count back in 5s to 5' and moves in an anti-clockwise direction three places (15, 10, 5).
- ❏ Player 2 picks a card that says 'Start at 46 and count on in 10s to 96' (56, 66, 76, 86, 96) and moves in a clockwise direction five spaces.
- ❏ Player 3 picks a card that says 'Start at 13 and count on in 10s to 53', moves in a clockwise direction four spaces and lands on a collect so picks up 1p.

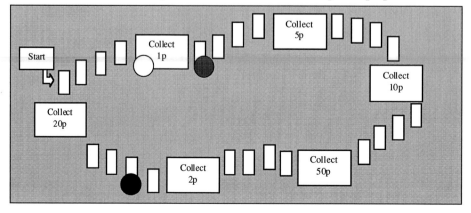

Example for Year 3 objective

❏ Use Game board 1 at first, but higher attainers could use Game board 3. You or the children can fill in amounts of money to collect.

❏ The same rules apply but only use the cards for counting on and back in 100s on the Cards 2 sheet, or mix these with the cards on the Cards 1 sheet as well.

Example for Year 4 objective

❏ Use Game board 2 or 3 (if the latter, write in appropriate amounts of money) and use the cards on the Cards 2 sheet, or mix these with Cards 1 for lower attainers.

Example for Year 5 objective

❏ Use Game board 2 or 3 and the cards on the Cards 3 sheet for counting on and back in 0.1s, 0.2s and 0.3s

Example for Years 6, 7 and 8 objectives

❏ Use Game board 3 filled in with appropriate amounts of money, writing those as decimals; for example £3.07. Use the cards on the Cards 3 sheet, using the blanks to include hundredths.

Variations

❏ The amounts of money on the 'collect' rectangles should vary according to attainment of the groups; for example, some Year 5 children may be able to find the coins to make 25p, 75p, £1.12.

Plenary session

❏ Go over same specific counting with targeted individuals to see who has understood the learning objectives and to assess specific skills.

❏ *'If I started at 125 and I had to count back in 25s, how many steps would I need to go to land on 75/50/25/zero?'*

❏ *'Going from 1,000 to zero, how many steps would it be if I counted in 1s/2s/5s/10s/50s/25s/100s?'*

❏ *'Count with me in steps of 0.3 from zero until we get beyond 5.'*

❏ *'What was new knowledge today for you?'*

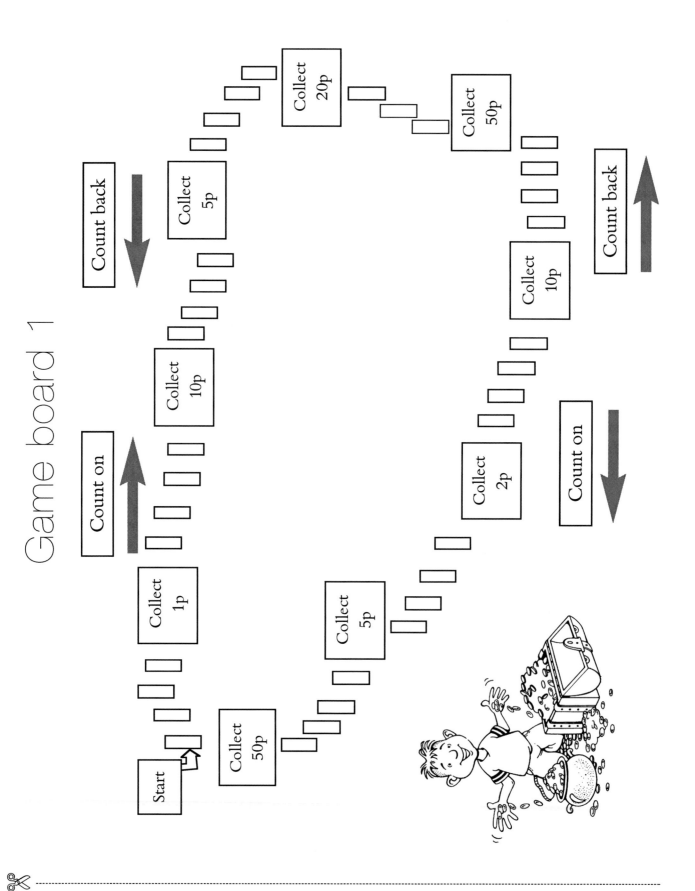

Game board 1

Count back

Collect 20p

Collect 50p

Count back

Collect 5p

Collect 10p

Count on

Collect 10p

Collect 1p

Count on

Collect 2p

Collect 5p

Start

Collect 50p

✂ --

Notes for teachers: This game board is for use with the Years 2, 3 and 4 objectives as suggested on pages 16 and 17. Photocopy onto A3 or A4 card.

Game board 2

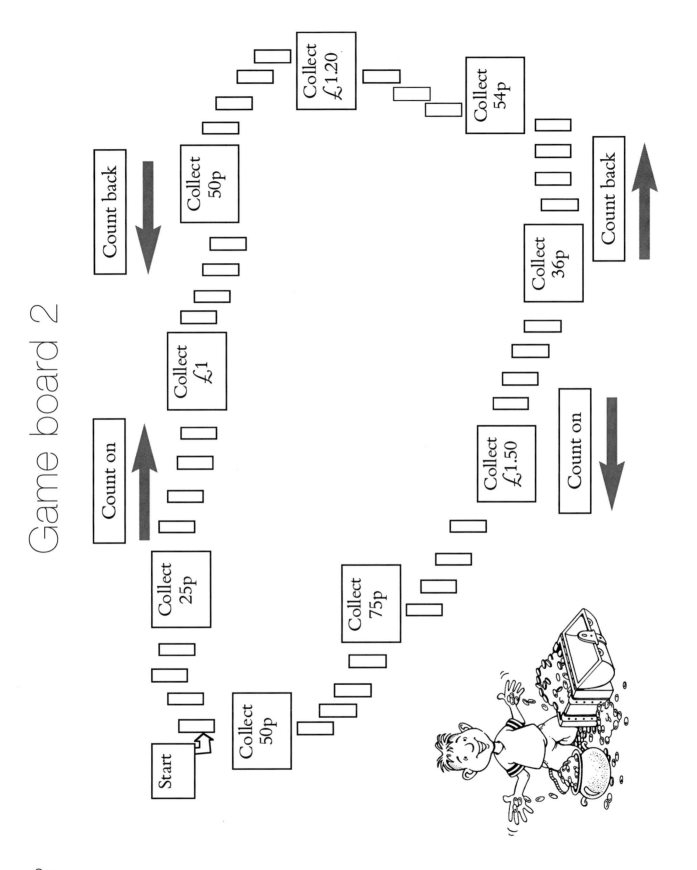

Start

Collect 25p

Count on

Collect £1

Collect 50p

Count back

Collect £1.20

Collect 54p

Count back

Collect 36p

Count on

Collect £1.50

Collect 75p

Collect 50p

Notes for teachers: This game board is for use with the Years 5 and 6 objectives as suggested on page 17. Photocopy onto A3 or A4 card.

Game board 3

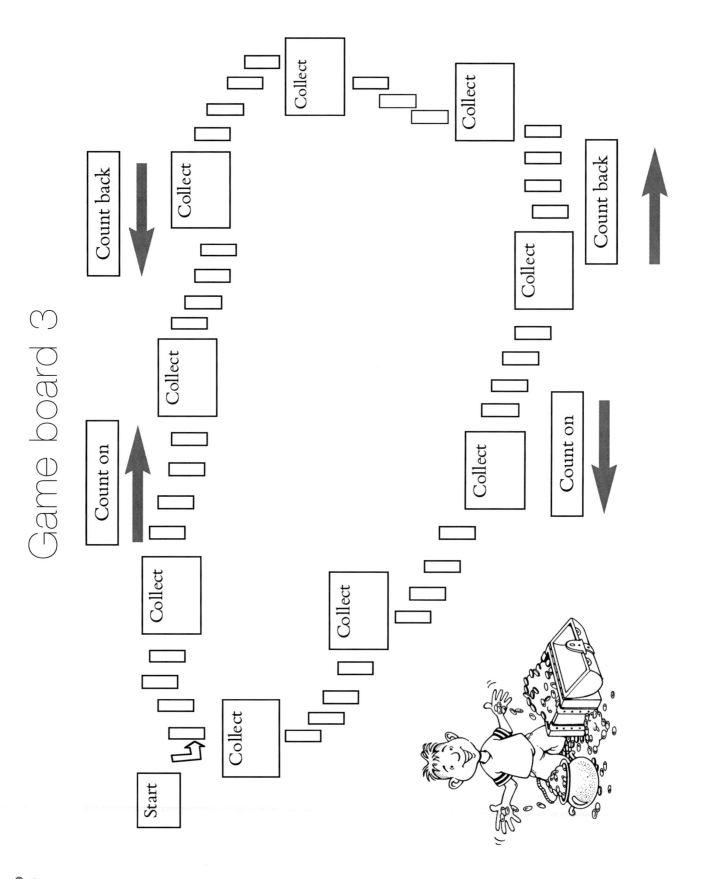

Start · Collect · Count on · Collect · Count back · Collect · Collect · Collect · Count back · Collect · Count on · Collect

Notes for teachers: This blank track can have 'collect' amounts, you or the children choose. Photocopy onto A3 or A4 card.

Cards 1

Start at 10 and count on in 5s to 40	Start at 15 and count on in 5s to 35	Start at 3 and count on in 10s to 33
Start at 85 and count back in 5s to 50	Start at 20 and count back in 5s to 0	Start at 6 and count on in 2s to 18
Start at 80 and count back in 10s to 50	Start at 48 and count back in 10s to 8	Start at 70 and count back in 10s to 10
Start at 20 and count back in 2s to 6	Start at 40 and count back in 2s to 30	Start at 20 and count on in 2s to 12
Start at 0 and count on in 5s to 25	Start at 8 and count back in 2s to 25	Start at 30 and count back in 5s to 15
Start at 25 and count on in 10s to 65	Start at 40 and count on in 5s to 65	Start at 16 and count on in 2s to 24
Start at 45 and count back in 10s to 15	Start at 28 and count on in 10s to 38	

✂ ---

Notes for teachers: Photocopy onto A3 or A4 and cut out. Use for Years 2 and 3 objectives.

Cards 2

Start at 400 and count back in 100s to 200	Start at 800 and count back in 100s to 400
Start at 200 and count on in 100s to 600	Start at 700 and count back in 100s to 100
Start at 75 and count back in 25s to 0	Start at 100 and count on in 100s to 400
Start at 125 and count back in 25s to 50	Start at 500 and count on in 100s to 800
Start at 100 and count back in 25s to 25	Start at 150 and count back in 25s to 75
Start at 0 and count on in 100s to 900	Start at 75 and count on in 25s to 300
Start at 0 and count on in 25s to 75	Start at 50 and count on in 25s to 175
Start at 500 and count back in 100s to 0	Start at 0 and count on in 25s to 25

Notes for teachers: Photocopy onto A3 or A4 and cut out. Use for Years 3, 4 and 5 objectives.

Cards 3

Start at 4 and count back in 0.1s to 3	**Start at 3 and count back in 0.1s to 1.8**	
Start at 12 and count on in 0.1s to 12.5	**Start at 12 and count back in 0.5s to 11.5**	
Start at 15 and count on in 0.1s to 15.6	**Start at 50 and count on in 0.5s to 55.5**	
Start at 20 and count on in 0.1s to 21.2	**Start at 10 and count back in 0.5s to 3**	
Start at 2 and count on in 0.1s to 2.7	**Start at 25 and count on in 0.5s to 27.5**	
Start at 12 and count on in 0.5s to 15.5	**Start at 20 and count back in 0.5s to 12**	
Start at 1 and count back in 0.1s to 0	**Start at 20 and count back in 0.5s to 17.5**	
Start at 12 and count on in 0.5s to 14	**Start at 10 and count back in 0.1s to 9.2**	

✂ ---

Notes for teachers: Photocopy onto A3 or A4 and cut out. Use for Years 5, 6, 7 and 8 objectives.

Aliens

Counting in different-size steps

This game is mainly about counting on, but challenge children to make a version that involves counting back.

A game for two to four players

Learning objectives

Year 2: Counting on in steps of 1, 2, 5 and 10.
Year 3: Counting on in steps of 10, 100, 2, 5, 3, 4.
Year 4: Counting on in steps of 25, 100.
Year 5: Counting on in steps of 25, 100, 1,000, 0.1, 0.2, 0.3.
Years 6, 7 & 8: Counting on in steps of 0.5, 0.25 and other hundredths, for example 0.35.

What you need

- a game board (page 26)
- spinners from Generic sheet 2 or make game cards using the blanks on Generic sheet 1
- counters
- children's rules (page 81)

How to play

The object is to be the first to cover all the aliens on the game board by answering a number question and covering the answer on the board. So, for a game where the players are answering questions on 'lots of 2', the board could have aliens with every even number from 4 to 26 written on them (there can be repeated numbers). The players spin the spinner, do the calculation and cover the answer on the board if they can. The first to cover all the numbers is the winner.

Introducing the game

❑ Say to the children *Today you are going to learn to count on in different steps.* Using a large wall number line, demonstrate some of the steps, such as counting in 3s (3, 6, 9…), or in 100s (100, 200…). Depending on the attainment of the children, adapt and demonstrate the following instructions.

Example for Year 2 objective

❑ These children could count in a mixture of steps, such as 2s, 5s and 10s, using Spinners 1 and 2 on Generic sheet 2.

❑ Prepare the game board by writing on it multiples of 2, 5 and 10 up to 7 lots of those multiples. So, the 5s will go from 2 lots of 5, to 7 lots of 5. You will not have space for a complete set of each, which makes the game have an element of luck in it. So you might fill five of the aliens with 15, 20, 25, 30 and 35, another five with some of the multiples of 10 (20, 30, 40, 50, 60 and 70) and the rest with multiples of 2.

❑ Player 1 spins a 4 on Spinner 1 and 'steps of 2' on Spinner 2. This means 'Count on in 2s four times', so that player puts a counter on the alien with 8 on it.

❑ Player 2 spins a 6 on Spinner 1 and 'steps of 5' on Spinner 2. This means that player has to count in 5s six times and they put their counter on 30.

❑ Player 3 spins a 3 on Spinner 1 and 'steps of 10' on Spinner 2. They need to put their counter on 30 but it is occupied, so they cannot do anything.

❑ Player 1 spins 'Count on in 10s nine times'. There is no 90 on the board, so the next player continues.

❑ Player 2 spins 'Count on in 2s nine times'. There is no 18 on the board, so the next player continues.

❑ Player 3 spins 'Count on in 5s five times' and puts their counter on 25. And so on.

Example for Year 3 objective

❏ This group can play as for Year 2, but use Spinners 1 or 3 for the number of steps, and Spinner 4 for the sizes of the steps. So you need to write on the aliens numbers for the steps of 10 or 100 from 2 to 7 steps on Spinner 1 (a selection from 20 to 130) or appropriate numbers if you are using Spinner 3 (8 to 13 steps – a selection from 200 to 1,300).

Example for Year 4 objective

❏ Use the same rules but the children can use Spinner 1 with Spinner 5. This will help them to practise a range of steps, including steps of 25. So you need to fill in the aliens from 2 lots of 5 to around 7 lots of 100. You will only be able to fit in a selection of the numbers, so for the steps of 25 you might choose 75, 125, 150, 175 and so on. If you want to focus on counting in 25s, you could make the game only counting in 25 and just use Spinners 1 or 3 to decide on how many steps of 25.

Example for Year 5 objective

❏ Use the same rules as above but use Spinner 6 or Spinner 7 (Generic sheet 3) for counting in decimal steps.

Example for Years 6, 7 and 8 objectives

❏ For these children use any of the spinners for the steps and Spinners 8 or 9 for counting in 0.25s and 0.5s. You could fill in the blank spinner for whatever you want to focus on. Remember that children making their own game is a useful assessment activity (see Variations).

Variations

❏ Challenge children to make a counting-back version of the game! They would need to decide on a starting number to count back from. For example, if they choose counting back in steps of 0.25 and they choose to do it up to 10 lots of 0.25, the starting number for counting back could be 3, so when they count back 4 lots of 0.25 (2.75, 2.5, 2.25, 2.00) the 2 has to be covered.

❏ Any of the games above can be played on a blank game board, with the children writing in the numbers they spin rather than covering them. Then, when all the spaces are written on, play continues, but this time by covering each number, so again the game is won by the player with the most of their colour counters on the board.

Plenary session

❏ Use an OHP and acetate of the board game to play with the class. Ask the children who have played during the lesson to explain the rules. Divide the class into four teams to play. Make sure everyone gets involved in the counting.

❏ Say *'If I started at zero and was taking steps of 5, how many steps would I take to get to 45?'*

❏ *'Let's count together in steps of 1,000 from zero as far as we can go.'*

❏ Extend the counting to counting back as well as forward, for example *'Let's count in steps of 0.5 to 10 and then back again.'*

❏ Extend the counting to counting from any two-digit number, for example *'Let's count from 32 in steps of 100 up to 3,200 and then back again to 32.'*

Notes for teachers: Photocopy this board onto A3 or A4 card and write the appropriate numbers on the aliens.

Choose your column

Place value and partitioning

> This game helps children to explore aspects of place value including using decimals.

A game for two to four players

Learning objectives

Year 2: Know what each digit in a two-digit number represents, including 0 as a place holder, and partition two-digit numbers into multiples of 10s and 1s.

Year 3: Know what each digit represents, and partition three-digit numbers into multiples of 100s, 10s and 1s.

Year 4: Partition numbers into 1,000s, 100s, 10s and 1s.

Year 5: Know what each digit represents in a number with up to two decimal places.

Year 6: Know what each digit represents in a number with up to three decimal places.

Years 7 & 8: Understand and use decimal notation and place value.

What you need

- digit cards from 0 to 9 (Generic sheet 7)
- a bag
- a game board (pages 29 to 31)
- pencils
- spinners (Generic sheets 3 and 4)
- children's rules (page 81)

How to play

The game is to be played in pairs. For example, using Game board 1, with tens and units, the first player picks two digit cards (0–9) and makes the highest number they can out of them. So, if they pick a 4 and a 7 they can make 74. That player then spins the spinner to see what they must do with their number. For example, they spin +10 giving a total of 84. That player fills in their game board as follows:

Round	T	U	+ or −	end number	score 1 or 10
1	7	4	+10	84	

The digit cards are put back in the bag. The second player has a turn. When he or she has finished, write 10 in the score column for the player with the higher number and 1 for the player with the lower number. They do this ten times then count up their total score. The game can be played with 100s, 10s and 1s on Game board 2.

Introducing the game

❏ Say to the children *'Today you are going to learn what each digit in a number represents.'* Explain that the game will help to reinforce their understanding. Depending on their attainment, adapt and demonstrate the game first.

Example for Year 3 objective

❏ This group can use Game board 2 for 100s, 10s and 1s. Each player takes three cards (0–9) out of the bag. They make the highest number they can. For example, with 4, 2, and 0 you can make 420.
❏ They write their number on the grid. They then use Spinner 11 (Generic sheet 3) to see what they must do with their number, for example +100. They write their new number in the '+ or −' column, in this case 520.
❏ Whoever makes the highest number wins the round and scores 100. The other player scores 10.
❏ Repeat this a total of ten times.
❏ The overall winner is the player who has the highest score.

Example for Year 2 objective

❏ These children should play using Game board 1 and Spinner 10 (Generic sheet 3).

Example for Year 4 objective

❏ These children can play the game with Game board 3 using 1,000s, 100s, 10s and 1s. For lower achievers you might want to label all the columns (for example, TH, H, T, U) before you give out the sheets. (Note that the column headings are not marked so either you or the children need to do this.)

❏ They can use two sets of 0–9 cards and pick out four cards to make the highest four-digit number. For example, Player 1 picks 4, 3, 7 and 9 and makes 9743. They should use Spinner 12 (Generic sheet 3).

❏ The winner scores 1,000 and the loser scores 100.

Example for Year 5 objective

❏ The children can use two sets of 0–9 cards. They have to pick out three cards to make the highest (or lowest) two-digit number with one or two decimal places, depending on the rules you make. For example, Player 1 picks out 4, 3 and 1 and makes either 4.31 or 43.1. They use Game board 3 with the decimal points marked in the columns. (Note that the column headings are not marked so either you or the children need to do this.) They can use Spinner 13 to play the game.

❏ The winner scores 1 and the loser scores 0.1.

❏ A more advanced version of the game is to use two decimal places and Spinner 14.

Example for Years 6, 7 and 8 objectives

❏ These children use Game board 3 and two sets of the 0–9 cards and pick three or four of them out of the bag to make numbers with either three or four decimal places. For example, Player 1 picks out 5, 9, 8 and 2 and makes 9.852.

❏ They use Spinner 14 or make up a more complex one using Spinner 9 or 18.

❏ Give the children experience with making up their own game.

Variations

❏ As an alternative to digit cards, this game can also be played using dice.

❏ Try asking the children to make the lowest possible number.

❏ You or the children can write alternative rules using the blank rule sheet on page 88.

Plenary session

❏ Ask a few of the pairs of children who have been playing the game to demonstrate exactly what they have been doing.

❏ Make sure the children have added up their own score correctly.

❏ Give some problems that relate to the numbers being used. For example, say *Who can tell me what we get if we add 100 to 943?* Ask someone to come to the front and write the number on the board, using the correct columns.

❏ Make up some complex calculations; for example, *'Start with 47. Add 0.1, subtract 10, add 0.001, subtract 0.1'* and so on.

❏ *'What was the most interesting thing you did in maths today?'*

❏ *'What do you still find hard to understand?'*

Name: _____

Game board 1

Game 1

Round	T	U	+ or −	end number	score 1 or 10
1					
2					
3					
4					
5					
6					
7					
8					
9					
10					
			Total score		

Game 2

Round	T	U	+ or −	end number	score 1 or 10
1					
2					
3					
4					
5					
6					
7					
8					
9					
10					
			Total score		

Notes for teachers: For use with the Year 2 objectives.

Name:

Game board 2

Game 2

Round	H	T	U	+ or –	end number	score 10 or 100
1						
2						
3						
4						
5						
6						
7						
8						
9						
10						

Total score

Game 1

Round	H	T	U	+ or –	end number	score 10 or 100
1						
2						
3						
4						
5						
6						
7						
8						
9						
10						

Total score

Notes for teachers: For use with the Year 3 objectives.

Name: _____

Game board 3

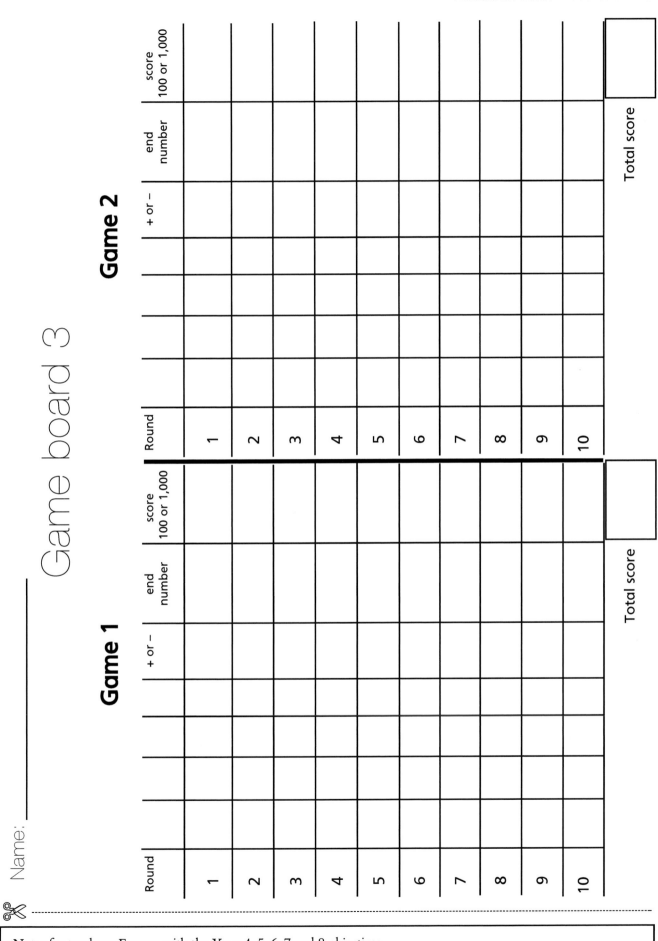

Game 2

Round	+ or –			end number		score 100 or 1,000		
1								
2								
3								
4								
5								
6								
7								
8								
9								
10								

Total score

Game 1

Round	+ or –			end number		score 100 or 1,000		
1								
2								
3								
4								
5								
6								
7								
8								
9								
10								

Total score

✂ --

Notes for teachers: For use with the Years 4, 5, 6, 7 and 8 objectives.

Game 5

Order, order!

Place value, comparing and ordering numbers

Vary this important game with digit cards, dice or spinners until you are sure children understand.

A game for two to four players

Learning objectives

Year 2: Know what each digit in a two-digit number represents; partition two-digit numbers into a multiple of 10s and 1s. Order whole numbers to at least 100.

Year 3: Know what each digit represents; partition three-digit numbers into multiples of 100s, 10s, 1s. Order whole numbers to 1,000.

Year 4: Partition numbers into 1,000s, 100s, 10s, 1s. Order whole numbers under 10 000.

Year 5: Know what each digit represents in a number with up to two decimal places. Order numbers with the same number of decimal places.

Year 6: Know what each digit represents in a number with up to 3 decimal places. Order a mixed set of numbers with up to 3 decimal places.

Years 7 & 8: Compare and order decimals.

What you need

- dice or digit cards (Generic sheet 7) or spinners (Generic sheets 2 or 4)
- a game board (page 34/35)
- pencils
- children's rules (page 82)

How to play

Each player needs their own grid. They take turns to throw two dice, take two digit cards or spin a 0–9 spinner twice to make the highest (or lowest) two-digit number they can. They write this number on their grid. This continues until all the grids are completed in one column. Then the children race to put the numbers they have made in order from smallest to largest. The winner is the player to order their numbers correctly first; the winner scores 10 points. Play the game several times and see who is the first to score 40 points.

Introducing the game

❏ Say to the children *'Today you are going to learn about the place value of numbers and ordering numbers.'* Depending on their attainment, adapt and demonstrate the game.

Example for Year 2 objective

❏ These children use a 1–6 dice, digit cards or Spinner 1 (Generic sheet 2) to make their two-digit number and record it on their own copy of grid 1.
❏ Player 1 gets the numbers 1 and 4 and so makes 41.
❏ Player 2 gets 2 and 5 and makes 52.
❏ Player 1 gets 6 and 4 and makes 64.
❏ Player 2 gets 3 and 4 and makes 43.
❏ Play continues until the grid is completed.

Race Time!

❏ The players order their numbers, writing the order either alongside the numbers or at the bottom of their grid. The winner of the game is the first to order them correctly.
Player 1: 21, 22, 41, 55, 63, 64
Player 2: 31, 42, 43, 52, 53, 64

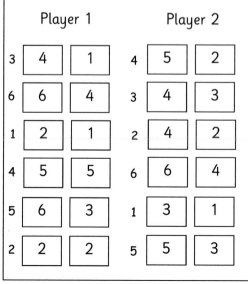

Example for Year 3 objective

❏ These children play the game as for Year 2, progressing to making and ordering three-digit numbers, which are recorded on Grid 2. Make sure they have had experience with using zero so they can use Spinner 15, numbered from zero to 9 (or use digit cards 0–9, putting the cards back after each go).

Example for Year 4 objective

❏ These children play the game as for Year 3, progressing to making and ordering four-digit numbers. They can use Spinner 15 (or digit cards) and can record on squared paper.

Example for Year 5 objective

❏ These children play the game as for Year 4, progressing to making and ordering two-digit numbers with one decimal place and single whole-digit numbers with two decimal places. Spinner 15 can be used here as well, and if you show the children how to put in a decimal point on Grid 2, they can record on that or on squared paper.

Example for Years 6, 7 and 8 objectives

❏ These children play the game as for Year 5, progressing to making and ordering numbers with three or four decimal places. Recording can be done on squared paper. Extend the game to using two-digit numbers and thousandths, perhaps by taking five digit cards from a bag (0–9) and putting the cards back each time.

Variations

❏ Play the game making the lowest number possible as well, writing alternative rules for Game 2 using the sheet on page 82 or use the blank rule sheet on page 88.

❏ Play as a whole class, timing the race to order the numbers. Play it again the next day to see if the ordering can be quicker.

Plenary session

❏ Check that the children have ordered their numbers correctly by passing round grids to be checked by others.

❏ Focus on problems any of them have had, such as ordering numbers like 4.512, 4.125 and 4.215.

❏ A fun (but noisy!) game is to make sets of cards for groups of children (for example, 1.24, 1.42, 2.14, 2.41, 4.12 and 4.21). Each child in the group has one card each. They race to get themselves in numerical order, holding their cards in front of them. Try the game the next day, giving a different set of cards to different groups and see if they can beat their time from the previous day.

Name: _____

Grid 1

Make the largest numbers that you can by throwing two dice.

Game 1		Game 2		Game 3		Game 4	

Race Time!
Order your numbers from smallest to largest. Write them below. The winner is the first player to finish. See how quick you can be.

ORDERING   Game 1 _____

Game 2 _____

Game 3 _____

Game 4 _____

Name: _____

Grid 2

Make the largest numbers that you can by throwing three dice.

Game 1			Game 2			Game 3		

Race Time!
Order your numbers from smallest to largest. Write them below. The winner is the first player to finish. See how quick you can be.

ORDERING   Game 1 _____

Game 2 _____

Game 3 _____

Game 6

Up, up and away!

Comparing and ordering numbers

This game can be played with any numbers.

A game for two to four players

Learning objectives

Year 2: Order whole numbers to at least 100.
Year 3: Order whole numbers to at least 1,000.
Year 4: Order a set of whole numbers less than 10,000.
Year 5: Order a set of numbers with the same number of decimal places.
Year 6: Order a mixed set of numbers with up to three decimal places.
Years 7 & 8: Compare and order decimals.

What you need

- digit cards in a bag (Generic sheet 7)
- a game board (page 38)
- pencils and paper
- water-based pens and a cloth
- place value cards (Generic sheets 5 and 6) or spinners (Generic sheet 4)
- children's rules (page 83)

How to play

The aim is to fill the game board with 10 two-digit numbers, the lowest at the bottom near the ground and the highest at the top beside the hot air balloon. Players take turns to take two digit cards and make a two-digit number. (They put the cards back in the bag.) They write their number on a piece of paper. They continue to do this until they have 10 numbers. When each player has 10 numbers, they race to put them in order and then write them on their game board. The winner is the player who completes their game board correctly first. They score 10 points. The game is played as many times as possible during the session. The overall winner is the child with the most points. (You might want to laminate the game boards and use water-based pens so they can be wiped clean.)

Introducing the game

❏ Tell the children that they are going to learn how to order numbers and that this game, for up to four players, will help to reinforce their understanding. Depending on their attainment, adapt and demonstrate the game.

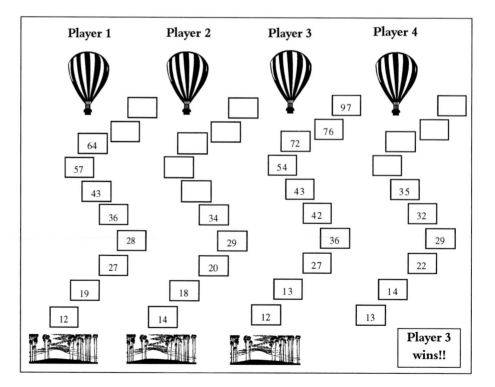

Example for Year 2 objective

❏ Player 1 takes two digit cards and makes a two-digit number such as 12. Player 2 does the same. Then Player 1 makes another number and so on until each player has made ten numbers. Player 1 ends up with the numbers 12, 36, 27, 87, 43, 89, 64, 28, 57 and 19, and has to put them in order. Once they are more confident the children could race to put them in order.

Example for Year 3 objective

❏ These players can take three digit cards to make three-digit numbers (or use place value cards, Generic sheets 5 and 6, putting them in three separate bags). They take turns to take one 100s, one 10s and one 1s card to make their three-digit numbers and then race to put them in order.

Example for Year 4 objective

❏ These children should make four-digit numbers and race to put them in order.

Example for Year 5 objective

❏ These children use two digit cards to make decimal numbers to one place, for example 3.6 and 4.2, and race to put them in order.

Example for Years 6, 7 and 8 objectives

❏ These players use three digit cards to make decimal numbers to 2 places, for example 4.35 and 2.16 and race to put them in order. They can then move on to using four digit cards to make decimals to three places.

Variations

❏ The game is to order the numbers, putting the smallest at the top.

Plenary session

❏ Ask the children to demonstrate what they have been doing, from making the numbers to ordering them. Call out 10 random two-digit numbers and ask the class to write them down and then order them in this way as quickly as they can.

❏ Say *'Imagine you are playing the game with only numbers up to 50. You have to write your two-digit numbers in the spaces when you first make them, not later. Where would you position 13/25/47?'*

❏ *'Which is larger, 2.16 or 2.61? How do you know?'*

❏ *'What did you find a bit tricky today? Do you need more practice at it?'*

❏ *'Make as many different numbers as you can with the three digits 2, 4 and 6. Now order them.'*

Name: _____

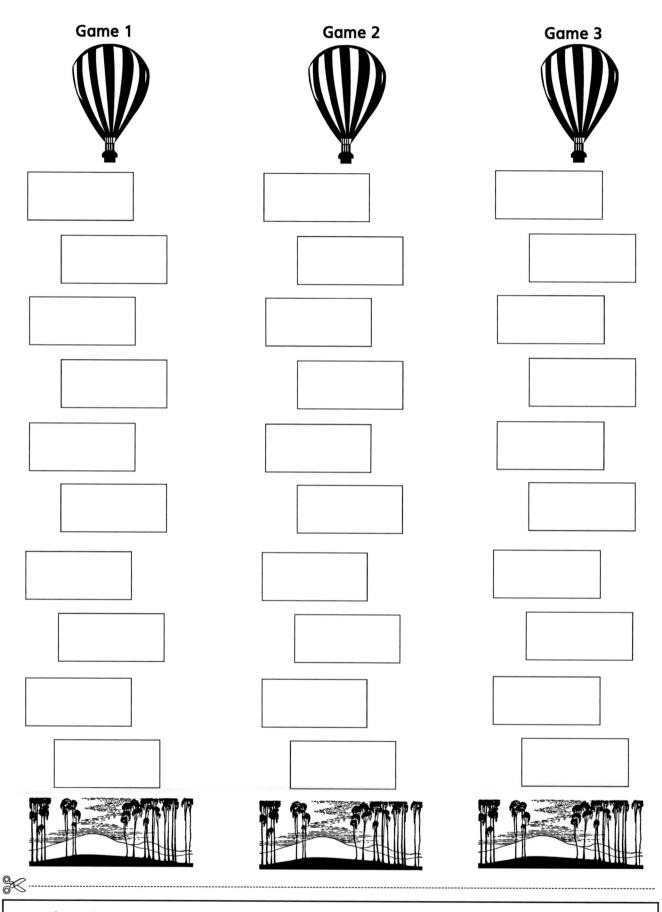

Game 1

Game 2

Game 3

✂ --

Notes for teachers: Photocopy this game board onto A3 paper or card and cut out.

Connect

Odd and even numbers

A game for two to four players

Learning objectives

Year 1: Begin to recognise odd and even numbers to around 20.

Year 2: Recognise odd and even numbers to at least 30.

Year 3: Recognise odd and even numbers to at least 100.

Year 4: Recognise odd and even numbers up to 1,000 and some of their properties, including the outcome of sums or differences of pairs of odd/even numbers.

Year 5: Make general statements about odd or even numbers, including the outcome of sums and differences.

Years 6, 7 & 8: Make general statements about odd or even numbers, including the outcome of products.

What you need

- dice and digit cards
- counters – one set of about eight of a colour each
- a game board (page 41)
- a large 100 square
- children's rules (page 83)

> This game can be used to help children to make generalised statements.

How to play

Players need to use either the grid on page 41 or one they have made themselves. They throw two dice and total the numbers thrown. If their answer is odd they cover a square with O in the middle, if their answer is even they cover a square with E. The aim of the game is to place four of their own counters next to each other in a row either horizontally, vertically or diagonally. The winner scores 10 points. They play again. The overall winner is the player with the most points at the end of the session.

Introducing the game

Tell the children that they are going to learn about odd and even numbers. Using a large 100 square, go over how to recognise odd and even numbers. If necessary remind them that even numbers end in 0, 2, 4, 6 or 8. Depending on the attainment of the children, adapt and demonstrate the game.

Example for Year 2 objective

(These children might find it helpful to have a large 100 square on display.)

- ❏ Player 1 throws 3 and 5, scores 8. Covers an E.
- ❏ Player 2 throws 1 and 1, scores 2. Covers an E.
- ❏ Player 3 throws 3 and 4, scores 7. Covers an O.
- ❏ Player 1 throws 2 and 6, scores 8. Covers an E.
- ❏ Player 2 throws 2 and 3, scores 5. Covers an O.
- ❏ Player 3 throws 6 and 5, scores 11. Covers an O.
- ❏ Player 1 throws 2 and 4, scores 6. Covers an E.
- ❏ Play continues until four of the same colour are in a row, vertically, horizontally or diagonally.

E	E	O	O	E	E
O	E	E	O	E	O
E	O	O	E	E	O
E	E	O	E	O	O
O	O	E	E	O	E
E	E	O	O	O	O

Example for Year 3 objective

❏ These children have to make up a two-digit number using the digit cards, and then throw a dice. They total the answer. So, for example, Player 1 takes cards 3 and 4 out of the bag. They make 34 with them, then throw the dice. The 3 lands face up so they add this to the 34 making 37 and cover the 'O' space on the board.

Example for Year 4 objective

❏ These children need to have investigated the outcomes of adding odd and even numbers together before playing this. They must predict whether their answer will be odd or even and explain why. For example, if 43 is made using the digit cards and a 5 thrown on the dice, they should be able to say that the answer will be even because when two odd numbers are added they always make an even number. After this the group playing should check by totalling the numbers. Only if the player was right in their prediction can a space be covered.

Example for Year 5 objective

❏ These children play the game as for Year 4 but use two sets of two-digit numbers made from digit cards, such as 36 + 27. This game has a bit more strategy in it and they must use their four digit cards in any order to get the number they need so that they can cover the 'O' or the 'E' on the board. For example, 36 + 27 will give an odd number, but 36 + 72 will give an even number.

Example for Years 6, 7 and 8 objectives

❏ The same basic rules apply, in that the players use two-digit numbers generated from digit cards and a dice. But as in the Year 5 game, they need to predict if the answer, when they multiply their two-digit number by the dice number, will be odd or even and explain why. The other players should check before allowing the space to be covered.

Variations

❏ The strategy aspect of the game (See Year 5) can be emphasised to higher achievers in all age groups. Let them make their first number by throwing a dice, then they must choose a digit card from a face-up pile to get the kind of number they want. So to cover an even space, 6 is thrown on the dice and the player chooses digit card 2.

❏ Let the children invent a subtraction game and use the blank rules sheet on page 88.

Plenary session

❏ Use an OHP and acetate of the board game to play with the class. Ask the children who have played during the lesson to explain the rules. Divide the class into four teams and play the game. Alternatively, play with two teams – you versus the class!

❏ Remind children to think of a strategy to win the game (see the Year 5 example).

❏ *Is 27 an odd or even number? How do you know?*

❏ *What kind of number do you get if you add an odd and an even number? Does that always happen, even with large numbers?*

❏ *What if you subtract an odd number from an even one?*

❏ *Tell me a general statement about adding an odd and an even number.*

Game board

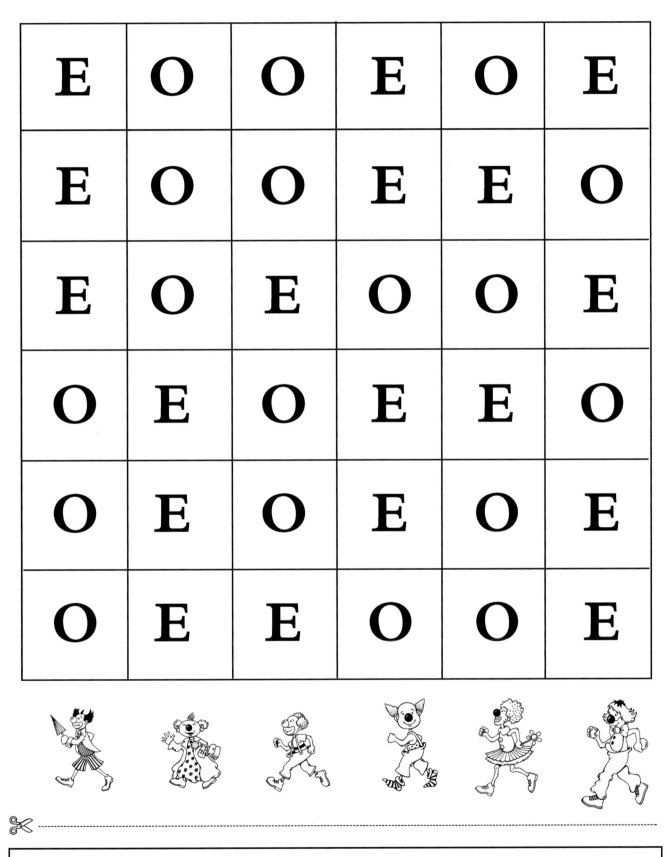

E	O	O	E	O	E
E	O	O	E	E	O
E	O	E	O	O	E
O	E	O	E	E	O
O	E	O	E	O	E
O	E	E	O	O	E

Notes for teachers: Photocopy this game board onto A3/A4 paper or card and cut out.

Game 8

Star trekking

Odd and even numbers

A game for two or three players

Learning objectives

Year 2: Recognise odd and even numbers to at least 30.
Year 3: Recognise odd and even numbers to at least 100.
Year 4: Recognise odd and even numbers up to 1,000 and some of their properties, including the outcome of sums or differences of pairs of odd/even numbers.
Year 5: Make general statements about odd or even numbers, including the outcome of sums and differences.
Years 6, 7 & 8: Make general statements about odd or even numbers, including the outcome of products.

What you need

- dice
- digit cards (Generic sheet 7)
- counters
- Unifix cubes or similar
- a game board (page 44)
- children's rules (page 84)

This game can be very easy or challenging, and the game board can be a basis for making up a new game.

How to play

Players use just one game board. They place their counters (which represent the crew of the space ship) on the start rectangle. They throw two dice and total the numbers. If the answer is an odd number they move on to a planet, if it is even they move onto a star. On the next throw, if their throw is even when the last throw was odd, they move their counter sideways onto the star track. If it is even again, they move one space towards the space ship. Play continues like this until they reach the space ship. When they get to the space ship they put a counter on the ship, so they have one crew member on the ship and start again with another crew member. The winner is the player with the most crew at the end of the session, and they can blast off into space.

Introducing the game

Tell the children that they are learning about odd and even numbers. It may be helpful to have a 100 square on display with the even numbers highlighted. Also have clearly displayed:

| odd ➡ planet | | even ➡ star |

Depending on the attainment of the children, adapt and demonstrate the following instructions.

Example for Year 2 objective

❑ Player 1 throws 3 and 5, scores 8 and places their counter on the first star.
❑ Player 2 throws 4 and 3, scores 7, and places their counter on the first planet.
❑ Player 1 throws 2 and 2, scores 4 and moves one space along the star track.
❑ Player 2 throws 3 and 1, scores 4 and moves sideways on to the even (star) track.
❑ Play continues like this.

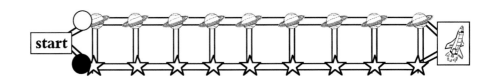

Example for Year 3 objective

❏ Make up a two-digit number using some digit cards and then throw a dice. Total the answer and then follow the example for Year 2. So, if digit cards 1 and 3 are picked out, making 13, and then a 2 is thrown, this makes 15 and the player moves on to the first planet.

Example for Year 4 objective

❏ The children need to have investigated the outcomes of adding odd and even numbers together before playing this version of the game. They must predict whether their answer will be odd or even and explain why. For example, if 43 is made using the digit cards and a 5 thrown, they should be able to say that the answer will be even because two odd numbers when added are always even. After this the group playing should check by totalling the numbers, and only if that player is right can they move.

Example for Year 5 objective

❏ These children play as for Year 4 but they should use two sets of two-digit numbers made from digit cards, for example 13 + 27. Introduce some strategies, such as encouraging the children to order the four digit cards to get the number they need.

Example for Years 6, 7 and 8 objective

❏ The same basic rules apply, using a two-digit number generated from digit cards plus a number thrown by a dice. The children need to predict if the answer, when they multiply their two-digit number by the dice number, will be odd or even and explain why. The group should check.

❏ Some children might be able to play by using any pencil and paper method to multiply two two-digit numbers together.

Variations

❏ Let the children make up their own rules for the game, for example allowing players to have two or more counters moving along the track. Strategy will be important here as one counter moving along the odd and another along the even will make the game quicker. The players can choose which of their counters to move each time.

❏ Challenge the children to use the game board to make up a game about three-digit numbers, or multiplying and so on, using the blank rules sheet on page 88 to record them.

Plenary session

❏ Ask the children to demonstrate what they have been doing by playing the game in front of the class, explaining what they are doing as they play.

❏ Ask *'Why will you win if you get several odd numbers in a row?'*

❏ *'How could you vary the rules a bit to make the game different?'*

Game board

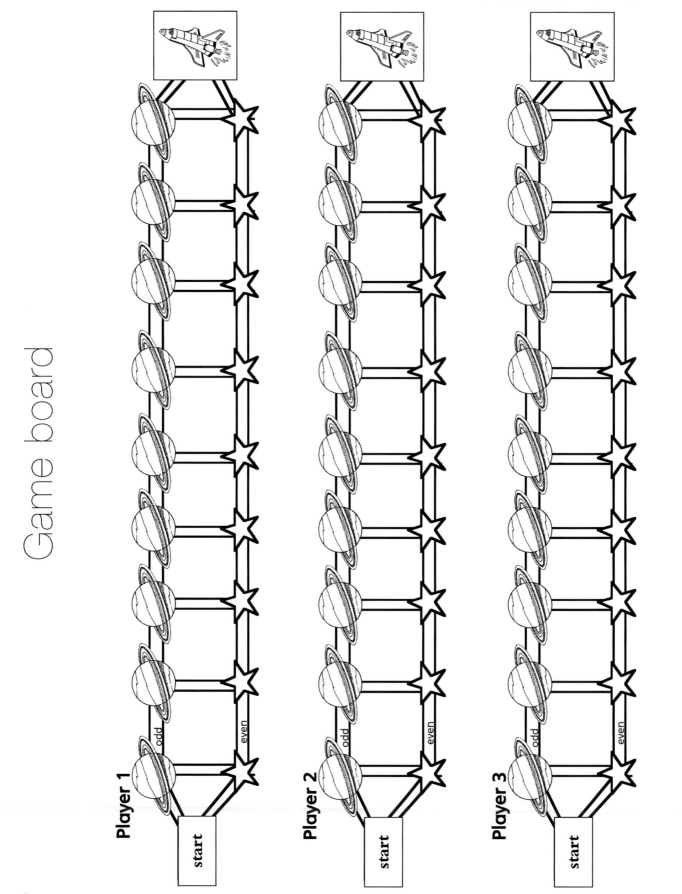

Player 1

start

odd

even

Player 2

start

odd

even

Player 3

start

odd

even

Notes for teachers: This is the Star Trekking game board for all objectives. Photocopy onto A3 paper or card.

Game 9

Round it!

Rounding

A game for two to four players

This game can be used to reinforce any shape work you have done.

Learning objectives

Year 2: Round numbers less than 100 to the nearest 10.

Year 3: Round any two-digit number to the nearest 10 and any three-digit number to the nearest 100.

Year 4: Round any positive integer less than 1,000 to the nearest 10 or 100.

Year 5: Round a number with one or two decimal places to the nearest integer.

Year 6: Round a number with two decimal places to the nearest tenth or to the nearest whole number.

Year 7 & 8: Round numbers, including to one, two and three decimal places.

What you need

- digit cards from 0 to 9 (Generic sheet 7)
- coloured counters, 10 of one different colour for each child
- a game board (page 47 or 48)
- children's rules (page 85)

How to play

Turn two or three sets of digit cards face down. Players take turns to pick two digit cards and make a two-digit number. They round their number to the nearest 10. If it matches a number in one of the shapes on the game board, the player covers it with a counter. If a number can't be covered, the next player takes their turn. The winner is the player with the most counters on the board. Replace the digit cards in exactly the same place each time.

Introducing the game

Tell the children that they are learning to round numbers to the nearest 10, 100, 1,000, tenth or hundredth. Depending on their attainment, adapt and demonstrate the following instructions.

Example for Year 2 objective

❏ Player 1 picks up 9 and 3 and makes 39. This is rounded to 40. A counter is placed on a number 40.
❏ Player 2 picks up 1 and 5 and makes 51. This is rounded to 50. A counter is placed on a number 50.
❏ Player 1 picks 4 and 5 and makes 54. This is rounded to 50. Another counter is placed on a trapezium.
❏ Player 2 picks 2 and 8 and makes 82. This is rounded to 80. A counter is placed on a rhombus.
❏ Play continues in this way. Eventually most of the shapes will be covered and it will become increasingly difficult to find an empty one, which will make it more exciting for the children.

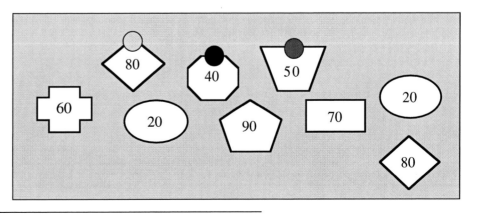

Example for Year 3 objective

❏ Play rounding to the nearest 10 as in Year 2, or fill the blank game board with 100s numbers, from 100 to 900. Players pick three digit cards and make a three-digit number. They round that to the nearest 100 and cover that number on the game board.

Example for Year 4 objective

❏ These children play the same game as Year 3 but begin to refer to the names of the shapes.

Example for Year 5 objective

❏ Write single-digit numbers in the shapes on the blank game board. Players pick two or three digit cards and, using a decimal point, make a number with tenths or hundredths to round to the nearest whole number. For example, Player 1 picks up 5 and 7 and makes 7.5, which is rounded to 8. A counter is placed on the shape with 8 inside it. Using three cards, Player 1 picks up 3, 5 and 7 and makes 3.57, which is rounded to 4. A counter is placed on the shape with 4 inside it.

Example for Years 6, 7 and 8 objectives

❏ The children play as for Year 5. Alternatively, fill the game board with tenths from 0.1 to 0.9. Players have to pick up two digit cards and, using a decimal point, make a number with hundredths to round to the nearest tenth. For example, Player 1 picks 6 and 9 and makes 0.69, which is rounded to 0.7. A counter is placed on the shape with 0.7 inside it. Extend the game to three places of decimals.

❏ Remember to use the correct terminology for the shapes.

Variations

❏ Try not returning each digit card to the same place, but mixing them up! This could be a slow game but it has a greater element of luck so lower achievers might score well.

❏ If you use one of the blank spinners, such as Spinner 9 on Generic sheet 3, filled in with six different shapes, the children could make their own game board, drawing around six different shapes. To play, the spinner is spun first and only a number on that shape can be covered, so digit cards need to be replaced carefully each time so that a number they want can be found.

❏ A slightly different game can be played in pairs where Player 1 gives Player 2 a number to round up or down to, such as 10 or 0.1 depending on the numbers being used. Play with at least two sets of digit cards to make sure there are enough zeros. So, playing with Year 6 rules, if Player 1 says to round to 0.1, Player 2 must pick up three digit cards, such as 0.08. That player can score ten points.

Plenary session

❏ Give focused questions to individuals to check what they have understood. For example, *Jake, read this number to me.'* (Write on the board 0.18 or to suit your children.) *'If you were rounding to the nearest whole number, what would that number be?'* (Zero). *'If you were rounding to the nearest tenth what would that number be?'* (0.2)

❏ *'Is there anything about rounding that you still don't understand or need more practice with?'*

❏ *'Why do you think rounding is important?'*

❏ *'When do you think we might use rounding in real life?'*

Game board 1

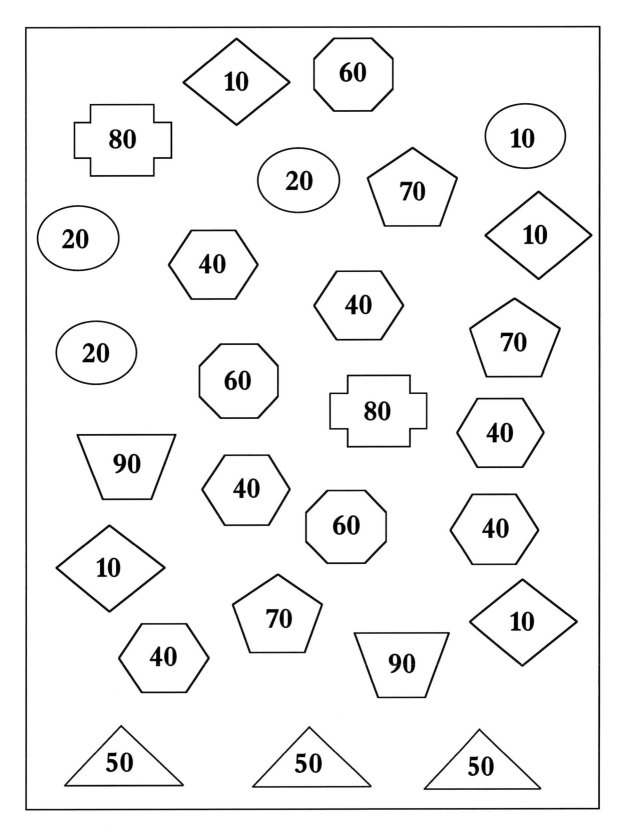

Game board 2

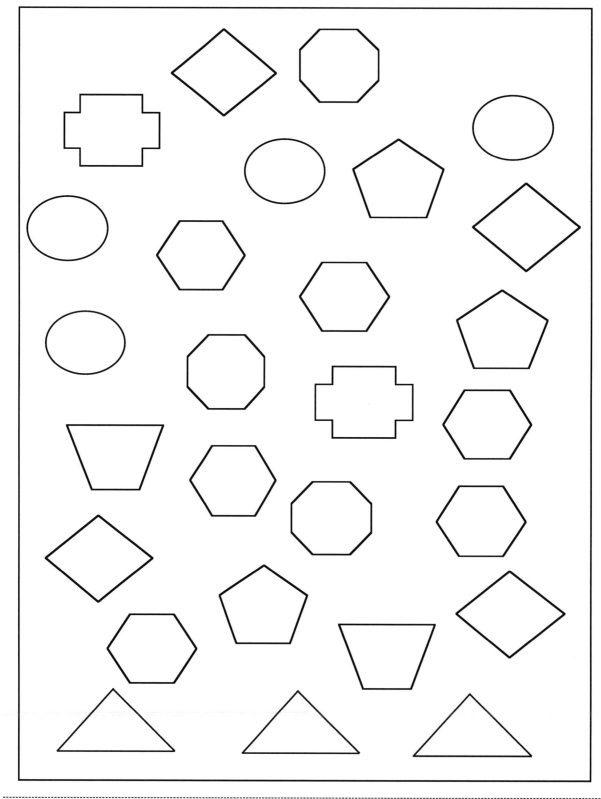

Notes for teachers: This is a blank game board for you or the children to fill in with their own numbers. Photocopy this game board onto A3 paper or card and cut out.

Four in a line

Rounding

A game for two or three players

This same game board can be used with a range of different numbers and rules, for example for either addition or multiplication.

Learning objectives

Year 2: Round numbers less than 100 to the nearest 10.

Year 3: Round any two-digit number to the nearest 10 and any three-digit number to the nearest 100.

Year 4: Round any positive integer less than 1,000 to the nearest 10 or 100.

Year 5: Round a number with one or two decimal places to the nearest integer.

Year 6: Round a number with two decimal places to the nearest tenth or to the nearest whole number.

Year 7 & 8: Round numbers, including to one, two and three decimal places.

What you need

- digit cards from 1 to 9 (Generic sheet 7)
- a '0' digit card per child
- coloured counters
- a game board (pages 51 to 53)
- children's rules (page 86)

How to play

Each player has a zero digit card. They take turns to pick a digit card (face down for a more difficult game) and put it beside their zero digit card to make a two-digit number. For example, one player picks 4 and puts it beside their 0 to make 40. They then need to look on the game board to find a number that can be rounded to it, such as 37 or 42. They place a counter on that number, put the digit card back (exactly where it was if you are playing with cards face down) and the next player has their turn. If there is no number available, the next player takes their turn. Play continues until one player has four counters in a row, either horizontally, vertically or diagonally.

Introducing the game

Tell the children that they are learning to round numbers to the nearest 10, 100, 1,000, tenth or hundredth. Many of them might know the rules of 'Connect Four' so will be familiar with the game.

Example for Year 2 objective

❑ Fill in the blank game board (page 53) with 2 digit numbers as in this example.

❑ Player 1 (red) picks up 3, puts it with 0 to make 30, chooses to cover 29.

❑ Player 2 (yellow) up picks 3, makes 30, covers 27.

❑ Player 3 (green) picks up 9, makes 90, covers 91.

❑ Player 1 picks up 4, makes 40, covers 36.

❑ Player 2 picks up 5, makes 50, covers 48.

❑ Player 3 picks up 6, makes 60, covers 62.

❑ Player 1 picks up 6, makes 60, covers 58.

❑ Player 2 picks up 7, makes 70, covers 72.

❑ Player 3 picks up 5, makes 50, covers 49.

❑ Player 1 picks up 8, makes 80, covers 84.

❑ Player 2 picks up 2, makes 20, covers 19 AND WINS!

27	29	36	47	54	67
34	19	51	83	16	21
12	17	48	49	84	69
26	23	62	72	58	43
78	24	39	59	78	51
91	33	41	94	71	63

Example for Years 3 and 4 objectives

❑ These children should play on Game board 1 with HTU numbers and use two digit cards face up to put with the zero to make a 100s number to round to. For example, someone makes 750 so the number on the board that can be rounded to 750 is 752. There may be no numbers to round it to, in which case the next player takes their turn.

Example for Year 5 objective

❑ These players should play on Game board 2 which has decimal numbers to one place. Ask the children to pick a single digit (no zero) to round to, so if a 4 is picked, the player can cover 4.3.

Example for Years 6, 7 and 8 objectives

❑ Fill the blank game board with numbers to two decimal places, such as 2.34, 5.25. Ask the children to pick a single digit to choose numbers to round to. So, if a 2 was picked they might choose 2.34. You can extend this game to three places of decimals and ask the children how they might fill in the blank game board for that game.

Variations

❑ The game can be played with spinners or dice to generate the numbers, such as Spinner 15 on Generic sheet 4. If a zero is not needed (for example, for Year 5) the players can spin again if they get zero first time or fill in numbers on spinner 18.

❑ The blank game board (page 53) can be used in a range of different ways, such as throwing two 1–6 dice and multiplying the two numbers to cover numbers.

❑ Challenge the children to make up their own game with learning objectives you give them, writing the rules on page 88.

Plenary session

❑ *What did you learn today? What was hard? Did anything surprise you?'*

❑ *'Tell me what you think the rules are for rounding numbers to the nearest ten/hundred, tenth etc.'*

❑ *'If you had to explain this rounding game to a child much younger than you, what would you say?'*

❑ *'Why do you think rounding is important? If you measured a bay in your room for three shelves and you went off to the shop for the wood, suggest what you might write down for your measurement.'* (Try to get to the idea that the bay might be 1m 79cms wide but you would be likely in your head to have rounded that up to about 1.80m so be buying an amount of wood rounded up to what you want. For three shelves you need about 5m 40cms, but you might have to buy 6 metres because the shop would sell planks in rounded-up amounts.)

Game board 1

127	279	356	427	594	667
304	189	591	823	176	211
172	317	458	479	814	659
226	293	682	752	528	423
738	254	390	592	785	517
391	332	241	914	721	643

✂ --

Notes for teachers: Photocopy this game board onto A3/A4 paper or card and cut out.

Game board 2

2.7	2.9	3.6	4.7	5.4	6.7
3.4	1.9	5.1	8.3	1.6	2.1
1.2	1.7	4.8	4.9	8.4	6.9
2.6	2.3	6.2	7.2	5.8	4.3
7.8	2.4	3.9	5.9	7.8	5.1
9.1	3.3	4.1	9.4	7.1	6.3

Notes for teachers: Photocopy this game board onto A3/A4 paper or card and cut out.

Game board 3

Notes for teachers: Fill in your own numbers. Photocopy this game board onto A3/A4 paper or card and cut out.

Game 11

Climb the ladder

A game for two to four players

Learning objectives

Year 2: Order whole numbers to at least 100.

Year 3: Order whole numbers to at least 1,000.

Year 4: Order a set of whole numbers less than 10,000.

Year 5: Order a set of numbers with the same number of decimal places.

Year 6: Order a mixed set of numbers with up to 3 decimal places.

Years 7 & 8: Compare and order decimals.

What you need

- a game board (page 56)
- number cards (pages 57 to 61)
- pencils
- Generic sheet 1
- Generic sheets 5, 6 or 7
- children's rules (page 86)

Ordering

> This game gives children experience with ordering numbers and there is a large element of luck in the game so lower achievers can often do well.

How to play

Players must know in advance whether they are using a complete set of numbers or a selection from a range of numbers, and the range of those numbers. Players are given a collection of two-digit numbers and have to fill the ladder with them in order, the highest number at the top. They take turns to take a number card from a face-down pile and decide where to put this number on their ladder. If they have more than ten numbers the game becomes more difficult because, if the range is 0–20 and they turn over a 7, they need to decide where is the best place for that number on the ladder, which only has ten spaces between rungs. After a number is placed it cannot be moved. If a number won't fit, it goes on the fire engine. The first to complete their ladder climbs up and wins the game and scores ten points. Players can play again to see who gets the most points.

Introducing the game

Tell the children that this is a game that will help them to learn to order numbers. Practise identifying middle numbers in a range, which could be 0–20, 0–100, 0.001–0.09 or whatever you are using. First order some cards you have prepared on a washing line or number line and then show the children how you can order them like a ladder with the lower numbers at the bottom and the higher ones at the top. Remind children who seem to be struggling, about the columns we use for numbers (THTU) and the decimal columns to thousandths.

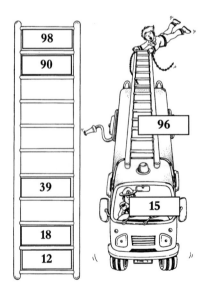

Example for Year 2 objective

❑ Tell these children the numbers they will be playing with, for example it could be a random selection of whole numbers from 0–100 (see page 57 for number cards for Year 2 or use Generic sheet 1 to make your own). Give each player a copy of the game board (page 56).

❑ Player 1 picks 39. This is less than half way so they place it quite near the bottom of their ladder. The other players take turns and put their numbers on their ladders.

❑ When Player 1 has a ladder filled in, for example as in the illustration on the facing page, if they turn over 96, it is not going to fit on the ladder so it is put on the fire engine.

❑ Winners of each game can score 10 points.

Example for Year 3 objective

❑ Use a selection of three-digit numbers from 100 to 1,000 (see the cards on page 58). Alternatively, make your own numbers using the blank cards on Generic sheet 1.

Example for Year 4 objective

❑ Use four-digit number cards (page 59), telling the children this is a random selection of numbers from (and including) 1,000 to 9,999.

Example for Year 5 objective

❑ Use the decimal and whole-number cards (page 60) telling the children that these range from and include, 0.1 to 10 to one place of decimals.

Example for Years 6, 7 and 8 objectives

❑ Use the decimal and whole-number cards on pages 60 and 61.

❑ Extend the game using the blank cards on Generic sheet 1 to make cards with a range of 0.011 to 1, using only numbers with three places of decimals, except for 1 as the only whole number. This game can have a much smaller range of numbers, such as from 0.001 to 0.1, and have several similar numbers, such as 0.010, 0.11, 0.001.

Variations

❑ Children can make a game for others to play. They could make it really difficult. For example, they could say to their friends that the cards are a selection of 30 from 0–100 and make a really unbalanced selection such as just 2, 7, 8, 9 and all the others higher than 70!

❑ Let the children investigate what will happen if they have a very wide range of numbers, such as all the numbers from 25 to 1,000 in steps of 25, or all the numbers from 0 to 100.

❑ The game can be played with place value cards (Generic sheets 5 and 6) 100s, 10s and 1s in different bags (for three-digit numbers). Players write their numbers on their game board, and write on the fire engine any numbers that won't fit on the ladder. Alternatively they can play with digit cards 1 (or 0) to 9 (see Generic sheet 7).

Plenary session

❑ *'How did you decide where to put your numbers? Were you good at guessing where to put numbers? Did you get any surprises?' 'Was there quite a bit of luck in your game or do you think it was mostly a game of skill?'*

❑ *'Which other numbers could have been in your set of numbers? Come and write them on the board.'*

❑ *'Which is larger 14 or 41 (or 0.41, 0.14 and 0.141)? How do you know? Could you explain that to a much younger child?'*

❑ *'How could you make a much more difficult game?'*

Number cards – 1

50	75	91
100	18	24
26	39	40
53	58	62
69	70	76
83	86	87
91	92	94

✂ --

Notes for teachers: Random two-digit numbers and 100 for Year 2 objectives. Photocopy onto A3/A4 paper or card and cut out.

Number cards – 2

150	275	491
100	108	124
261	399	400
539	589	602
659	700	761
863	865	872
901	912	943
967	980	1000

Notes for teachers: Random three-digit numbers and 1,000 for Year 3 objectives. Photocopy onto A3/A4 paper or card and cut out.

Number cards – 3

1500	2750	4910
9999	1085	1245
2619	3999	4000
5390	5899	6025
6591	7006	7615
8632	8653	8729
9010	9125	9437
9676	9999	1000

✂ ---

Notes for teachers: Random four-digit numbers for Year 4 objectives. Photocopy onto A3/A4 paper or card and cut out.

Number cards – 4

0.1	0.8	0.9
1.5	1.6	1.8
2.7	2.8	3.4
3.6	4	4.1
5.2	5.5	5.7
6.4	6.8	7.2
7.6	8	8.3
9.4	9.9	10

✂ --

Notes for teachers: Random decimal number cards for Year 5 objectives. Photocopy onto A3/A4 paper or card and cut out.

Number cards – 5

0.11	0.87	0.99
1.52	1.68	1
2.75	2.84	3.42
3.61	4.23	4.16
5.25	5.58	5.7
6.45	6.89	7.2
7.67	8	8.34
9.41	9.99	10

✂ ---

Notes for teachers: Random decimal number cards for Years 6, 7 and 8 objectives. Photocopy onto A3/A4 paper or card and cut out.

Elephant estimating

Counting and estimating

This game gives practice in counting as well as estimating. Even children in Years 6, 7 and 8 can find counting a large number of items quite challenging.

A game for two to six players

Learning objectives

Year 1: Give a sensible estimate of a number of objects, up to 30.

Year 2: Give a sensible estimate of up to 50 objects.

Year 3: Give a sensible estimate of up to about 100 objects.

Year 4: Make and justify estimates of up to about 250.

Year 5: Make and justify estimates of large numbers.

What you need

- a game board (one elephant per player) from page 64
- cubes or counters
- pencils and paper
- number lines
- children's rules (page 87)

How to play

Establish the size and number of objects the children can hold in their hands. For example, for estimating numbers up to 30 you might use Unifix cubes so that they can take two handfuls to get a quantity of cubes in the 20s. You could use acorns, buttons, small counters or plastic pennies for work with larger numbers.

One player takes a handful (or more) of objects and drops them carefully on the table so that they spread out. Each player has to immediately estimate (not count) how many cubes there are (anyone who counts is disqualified from that round). They then write down their estimates and show them to each other. As a group, they count the cubes. The player (or players) with the closest estimate wins a counter to put on their elephant game board. (You might find a number line useful here.) The overall winner is the player with the most counters on their elephant at the end of the session.

Introducing the game

Tell the children that they are learning to estimate quantities. Give some examples. For example, have some sweets in a clear jar or show a packet of something such as a see-through pack of raisins and ask for estimates. Say that during the game they will be penalised if they count before everyone has estimated! Explain that it is acceptable to get an estimate wrong and you will be deeply suspicious of people who keep getting exact estimates because they are probably counting! No-one gets every estimate right.

Revise with the children how to count carefully. Encourage them to move from the inefficient counting in 1s that the very young do.

1. Count the cubes in 2s, moving them as they are counted so that it is clear which cubes have been counted and which haven't.
2. Put the cubes in groups of 10. (Later in 100s.) Then count how many groups there are and how many left over.
3. Check the count. Everyone should agree on how many!

Example for Year 1 objective

❏ One player takes two handfuls of cubes and drops them carefully on the table. Player 1 estimates 20, Player 2 estimates 25, Player 3 estimates 30 and Player 4 estimates 27. They write these down. The cubes are counted carefully and there are 26. Players 2 and 4 are closest and put a counter on their elephants.

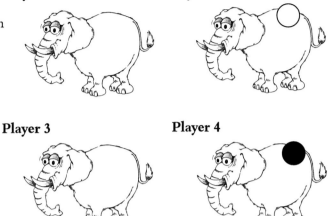

Player 1 **Player 2**

Player 3 **Player 4**

Example for Year 2 objective

❏ These children play the game as for Year 1 but estimating up to 50 small objects. (You might want to let them scoop up objects with a margarine pot for these larger quantities.)

Example for Year 3 objective

❏ As for Year 2 but estimating up to 100 small objects.

Example for Year 4 objective

❏ As for Year 2 but estimating up to 250 small objects and explaining to the group why they made that estimate. Make sure the children have enough desk space to put the objects in groups of 10, then 100. Emphasise that counting might seem easy, but actually you need to be very organised and have a system for checking. (One group could go and check the count for another group.)

Example for Year 5 objective

❏ As for Year 2 but estimating any number of objects and justifying to the group why they made their estimate. Extend the game with estimating other things, such as sweets in a jar, and discuss strategies for estimating. Even high achievers can find counting a large number of items requires problem-solving skills and cooperation they might not have anticipated!

Variations

❏ You can play the game without the game board and the children use a number line and/or pencil and paper calculations to work out how many points are scored. The player/s with the closest estimate scores zero. Other players score the number of points they are away from the counted total. So if 147 pennies are counted and a player has estimated 160, that player would score 13. The player with the lowest total at the end of the game wins.

Plenary session

❏ Prepare some OHP acetates or cards with stickers or blobs of the numbers your children are using and ask them exactly what they do first to estimate, then to count. You could leave these on display for a few days so that children can build up a mental image of what 'about 60', for example, looks like.

❏ Extend estimation skills to measuring. For example, *How heavy is the box?*, *How long is this piece of string?* and *How tall is Serena?*

❏ *What have you learned today about estimating? Do you feel confident with estimating up to 100 (and so on)? Would you like to try estimating up to a larger number?*

❏ *'Tell me something important about counting a lot of things.'*

Elephant game board

The approximation game

Estimating by approximation

A game for two to four players

> This game can be used to reinforce all kinds of calculations and calculation strategies.

Learning objectives

Year 4: Estimate and check by approximating (round to the nearest 10 or 100).

Year 5: Estimate by approximating (round to nearest 10 or 100), then check result.

Year 6: Estimate by approximating (round to nearest 10, 100 or 1,000), then check result.

Year 7 & 8: Make and justify estimates and approximations of numbers and calculations.

What you need

- a game board (page 67)
- calculation cards (page 68) or make your own using the blank cards on Generic sheet 1
- one counter per player
- a calculator
- number lines
- children's rules (page 87)

How to play

The calculation cards are placed face down on the table. Players pick a card, approximate the answer and explain how they did it. For example, Player 1 picks 72 – 63, decides the answer is around 10, explaining that 72 can be rounded to 70, 63 to 60, and 70 – 60 is 10. The other players use a calculator to find the correct answer, in this case 9, and work out how close the approximation was. Player 1 moves on that number of spaces on the game board, in this case 1. The winner is the last player to reach the 'Home' space, as this player will have had the closest approximations.

Introducing the game

Tell the children that approximating is like estimating but we tend to use rounding to get numbers that are quite close to the numbers you are dealing with, so 345 divided by 9 must be quite close to 345 divided by 10. Revise the kinds of calculations that you want to cover, showing the children how to approximate. For example, 99 x 3 is approximately 100 x 3. Where relevant, revise rounding to the nearest ten, hundred or whole number with decimals, or to the nearest tenth or hundredth for two and three places of decimals. With younger children and lower achievers you might find it helpful to use a number line to demonstrate the numbers. Say, *'We can round up 47 to 50 because 47 is close to 50.'* Go over some of the actual calculations you are using.

Example for Year 4 objective

- ❑ Use the calculation cards on page 68, which are subtractions, or use additions or whatever you want to practise using the blank cards on Generic sheet 1.
- ❑ Player 1 picks 51 – 32. They estimate 20 and explain. The actual answer is 19. They move one space along the game board.
- ❑ Player 2 picks 76 – 38. They estimates 40 and explain. The actual answer is 38. They move two spaces along the game board.
- ❑ Player 3 picks 157 – 98. Estimates 60 and explains. The answer is 59. They move one space along the game board.
- ❑ Player 1 picks 107 – 91. They estimates 20. The answer is 16. They move four spaces along the game board.
- ❑ Player 2 picks 166 – 119. They estimate 50 and explain. The answer is 47. They move 3 space along the game board.
- ❑ Play continues like this. The last one home wins.

Example for Year 5 objective

❏ Fill the blank calculation cards with three-digit or other calculations.

❏ Players approximate by rounding to the nearest 100.

❏ They might need to find the real answer by using a calculator, pencil and paper or a number line.

❏ They move along the game board the number of 10s that is the difference between their estimation and the answer. For example, 435 – 289. Estimate 100 because 435 is rounded to 400 and 289 is rounded to 300, so 400 – 300 is 100. The actual answer is 146, the difference is 46 so they move four spaces along the game board.

Example for Years 6, 7 and 8 objectives

❏ Fill the blank calculation cards with four-digit or other calculations.

❏ Players approximate the answer by rounding to the nearest 1,000.

❏ They might need to find the real answer by using a calculator, pencil and paper or a number line.

❏ They move along the game board the number of 100s in their estimation. For example, 2123 – 1489. Estimate 1000 because 2123 can be rounded to 2000, 1489 to 1000. So 2000 – 1000 is 1000. The actual answer is 634, the difference is 366, so they move 3 spaces along the game board.

Variations

❏ The game could be played with players just keeping a running total of their score rather than moving around the track. The player with the lowest score wins.

❏ Extend the game by challenging the children to make up their own rules for a game about approximating to two or three places of decimals. Use the blank rules sheet on page 88 to record them.

Plenary session

❏ The game can be played in four teams with you giving focused questions to particular individuals so that you can assess their attainment in calculating.

❏ Challenge the children to make up some calculations using the blank cards. If some of these turn out to be rather difficult calculations, ask why they are so difficult. (For example, if neither of the numbers round up or down well, such as 46 + 57. Would they round this to 50 + 60? That will give an approximation well over the actual total. Or would they round 46 to 45 rather than to a tens number? Or round 46 down to 40 and 57 up to 60?) Let groups see which strategy gives the closest total.

❏ *'Tell us one of your strategies you use for approximating.'*

❏ *'Why is it important to approximate before you do a calculation?'* (Encourage the children always to approximate! *'Can I do this in my head?'* needs to be the first response to being given a calculation.)

Game board

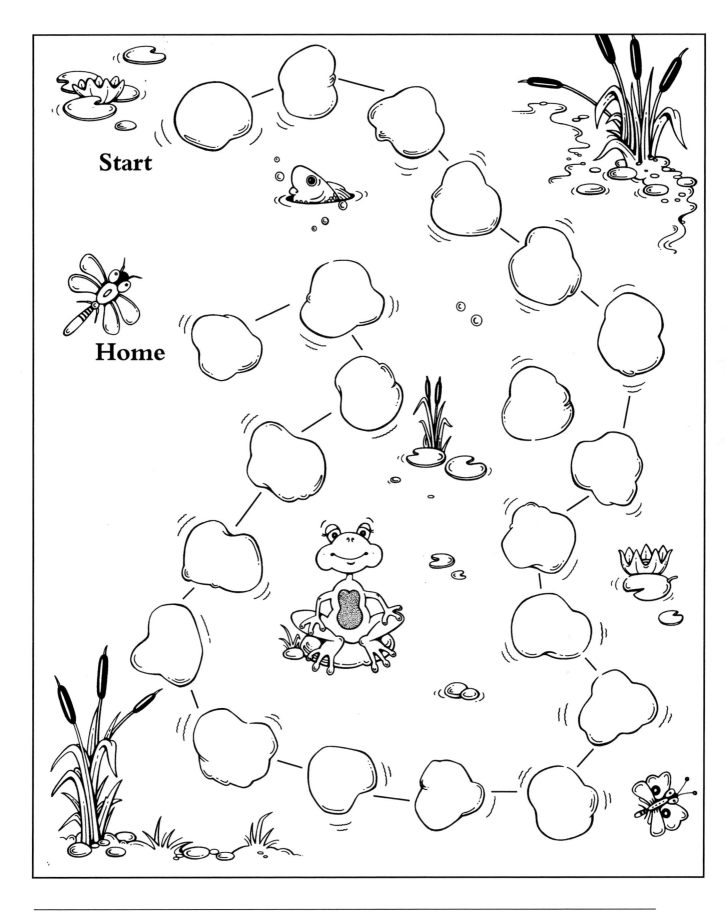

Start

Home

Calculation cards

98 – 71	87 – 61	51 – 32
79 – 51	99 – 48	67 – 39
83 – 71	98 – 79	47 – 29
97 – 38	67 – 18	90 – 37
49 – 38	91 – 82	92 – 31
37 – 18	57 – 39	53 – 29
57 – 39	91 – 62	72 – 63
47 – 18	31 – 12	82 – 34
87 – 48	84 – 38	76 – 38
107 – 91	138 – 109	129 – 82
117 – 69	166 – 119	157 – 98

Notes for teachers: Photocopy onto A3/A4 paper or card and cut out.

Bingo

Odd and even numbers

A game for the whole class or two to four players

Learning objectives

Year 2: Recognise odd and even numbers to at least 30.

Year 3: Recognise odd and even numbers to at least 100.

Year 4: Recognise odd and even numbers up to 1,000 and some of their properties, including the outcome of sums or differences of pairs of odd/even numbers.

Year 5: Make general statements about odd or even numbers, including the outcome of sums and differences.

Years 6, 7 & 8: Make general statements about odd or even numbers, including the outcome of products.

What you need

- blank cards (3 x 2, 3 x 3 or 3 x 4) from page 71
- pencils
- a 100 square
- children's rules (page 88)

> This game is shown using odd and even numbers as the learning objective but it can be used for many different objectives.

How to play

Players are given bingo cards and have to cross out numbers according to the criteria you give them. For example, you say *'All the even numbers between 3 and 7.'* They cross out 4 and 6 if they have them on their cards. If not, they don't cross any numbers out. Some questions will require them to look for one number, others two or more. The winner is the child to cross off all their numbers first.

Players could write in their own numbers on the cards. For example, you might say *'Write numbers on your card that are between 1 and 30.'*

If this game is to be played without adult support, select a group member to be the question caller. There are examples of questions to call out related to odd and even numbers on this and the next page.

Introducing the game

Tell the children how to mark their bingo cards. Practise the kinds of calculations you are going to use. For odd and even numbers you might want to keep a 100 square on display. If you are using children as callers help them to construct lists of what they will call, or choose children who can write quickly to act as callers. Stress the importance of keeping note of what they say and the need to check the winner's cards carefully.

Example for Year 2 objective

- ❑ Cross out the even numbers between 1 and 7. (None on this card.)
- ❑ Cross out the odd numbers with 5 in. (15 on this card.)
- ❑ Cross out the even numbers that are over 20. (24 on this card.)
- ❑ Cross out the odd numbers that are less than 10. (3 on this card.)
- ❑ Cross out the odd numbers that come when you count in 5s. (15 on this card – already crossed out.)

24	12	15
16	3	10

- ❑ Cross out the even numbers that come when you count in 10s. (10 on this card.)
- ❑ Cross out the odd number that tells us how many sides a triangle has. (3 on this card – already crossed out.)
- ❑ Cross out the even numbers between 11 and 17. (12 and 16 on this card.)

Example for Year 3 objective

❏ Use numbers up to 100. The following are possible questions for a card filled with numbers from 50 to 100.
1. Cross out the even numbers between 51 and 67.
2. Cross out the odd numbers with a 3 digit in.
3. Cross out the even numbers that are over 80.
4. Cross out the odd numbers that are less than 60.
5. Cross out the odd numbers that are multiples of 5.
6. Cross out the even numbers that are multiples of 10.
7. Cross out the odd numbers between 90 and 100.
8. Cross out the even numbers between 91 and 99.

Example for Year 4 objective

❏ Use numbers up to 1,000. The following are possible questions for a card filled with numbers from 500 to 1,000.
1. Cross out the even numbers between 515 and 600.
2. Cross out the odd numbers with a 7 digit in.
3. Cross out the even numbers that are over 950.
4. Cross out the odd numbers that are less than 600.
5. Cross out the odd numbers that are multiples of 5.
6. Cross out the even numbers that are multiples of 10.
7. Cross out the odd numbers between 900 and 1000.
8. Cross out the numbers that have an even tens digit.

Example for Year 5 objective

❏ As Year 4 but use appropriate vocabulary. The following are possible questions for a card filled with numbers from 200 to 600.
1. Cross out the even numbers between 415 and 441.
2. Cross out the numbers with an odd tens digit.
3. Cross out the even numbers that are less than 299.
4. Cross out the odd numbers that are less than 600.
5. Cross out the odd numbers that are multiples of 5.
6. Cross out the even numbers that are multiples of 10.
7. Cross out the odd numbers between 400 and 500.
8. Cross out the numbers that have an even hundreds digit.

Example for Years 6, 7 and 8 objectives

❏ Objectives for Year 6 (also appropriate for Year 7): as for Year 4 but use vocabulary appropriate to Years 6 and 7. The following are possible questions for a card filled with numbers from 0 to 1000.
1. Cross out the odd numbers between 0 and 150.
2. Cross out the numbers with an odd tens digit.
3. Cross out the numbers that are multiples of 10.
4. Cross out the odd numbers that are between 600 and 676.
5. Cross out the odd numbers that are multiples of 5.
6. Cross out the even numbers that are multiples of 25.
7. Cross out the odd numbers that are greater than 950.
8. Cross out the numbers that have an even hundreds digit.

Variations

❏ If you wanted to focus on place value of three-digit numbers, the children could write on their cards any three-digit numbers and you can call out: '1. *Any number with three hundreds. 2. Any number with seven tens,*' and so on.
❏ To give more practice with rounding, they can write any two/three-digit number on the card and you can call out: '1. *Any number that rounds to 60. 2. Any number that rounds to 100,*' and so on.

Plenary session

❏ Ask the children what might be suitable questions for a learning objective you choose. For example, if you wanted to cover ordering decimals, questions might be '*Cross out any numbers larger than 0.5*' and so on. Play the game as a whole class often. Children love it!

Blank bingo cards

Spinner 1   Spinner 2 (Year 2/3)

Spinner 3   Spinner 4

Spinner 5   Spinner 6

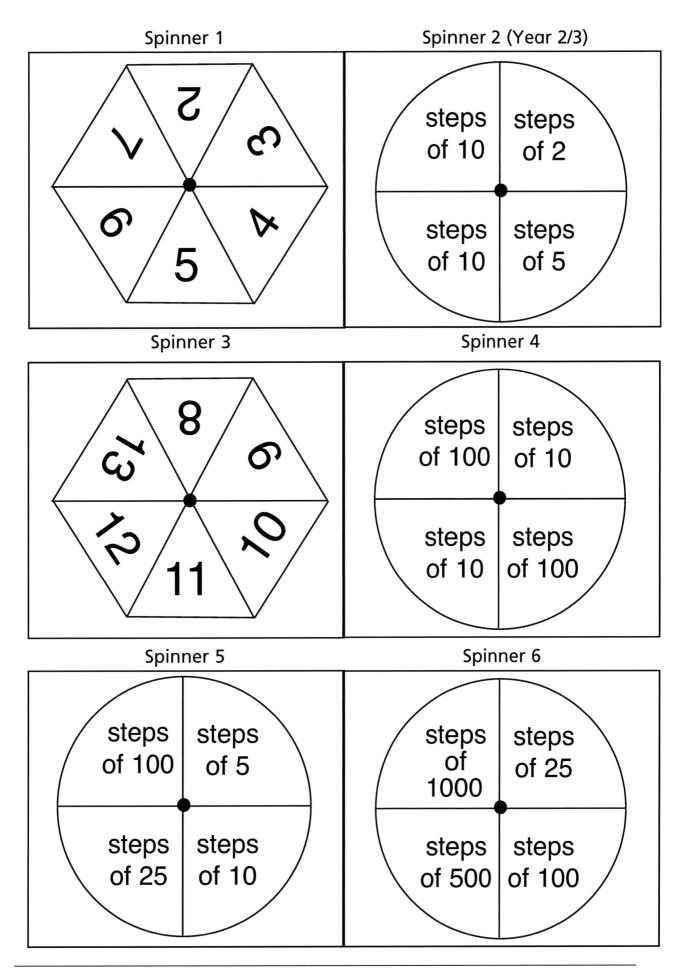

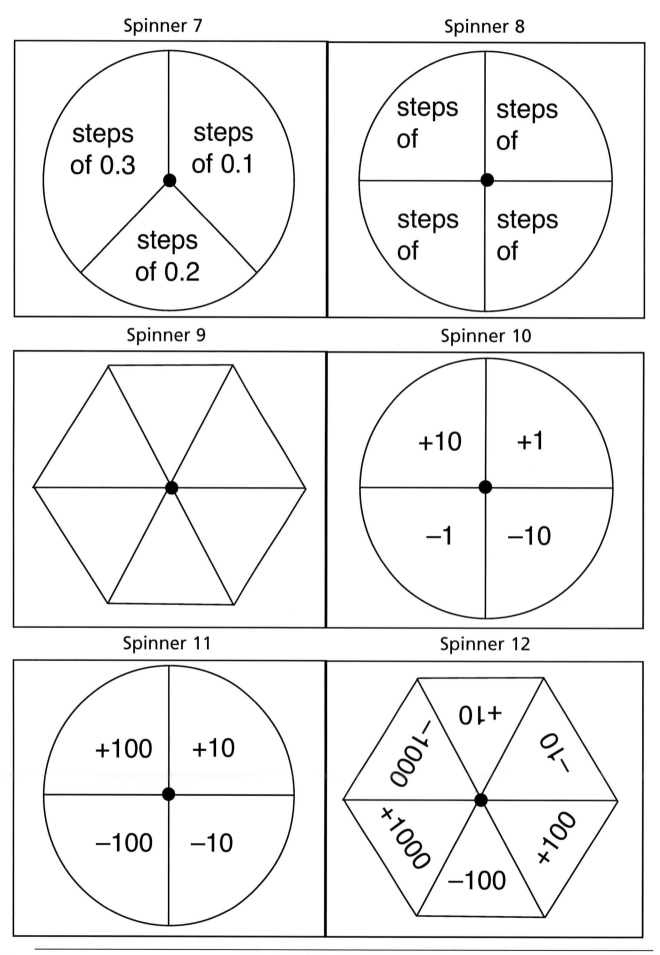

Spinner 7

steps of 0.3 | steps of 0.1 | steps of 0.2

Spinner 8

steps of | steps of | steps of | steps of

Spinner 9

Spinner 10

+10 | +1 | −1 | −10

Spinner 11

+100 | +10 | −100 | −10

Spinner 12

+10 | −10 | −1000 | +100 | +1000 | −100

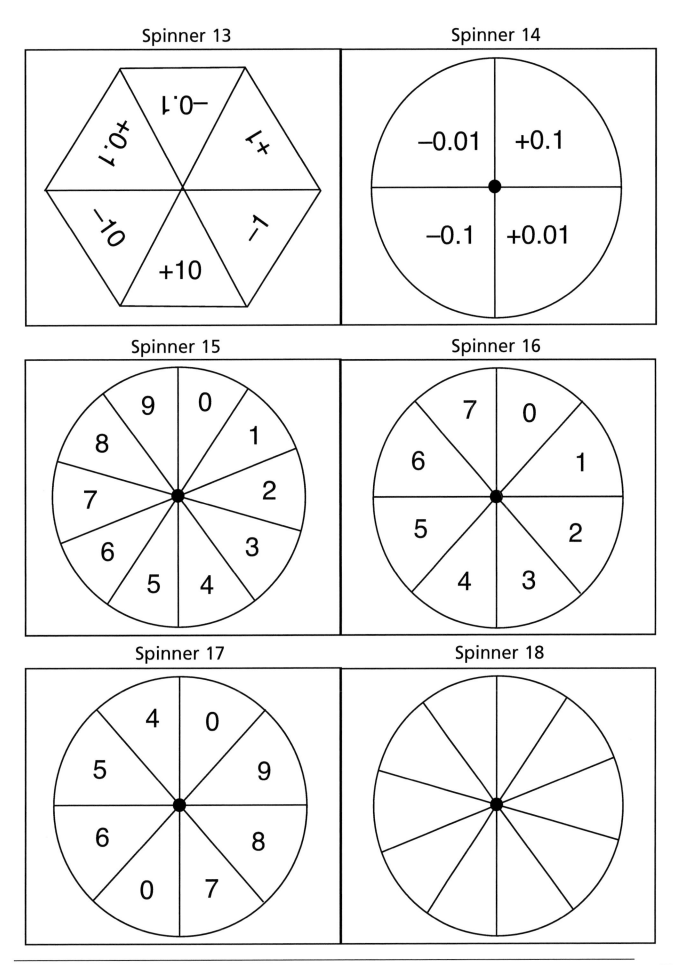

Spinner 13

Spinner 14

Spinner 15

Spinner 16

Spinner 17

Spinner 18

Place value cards

Place value cards

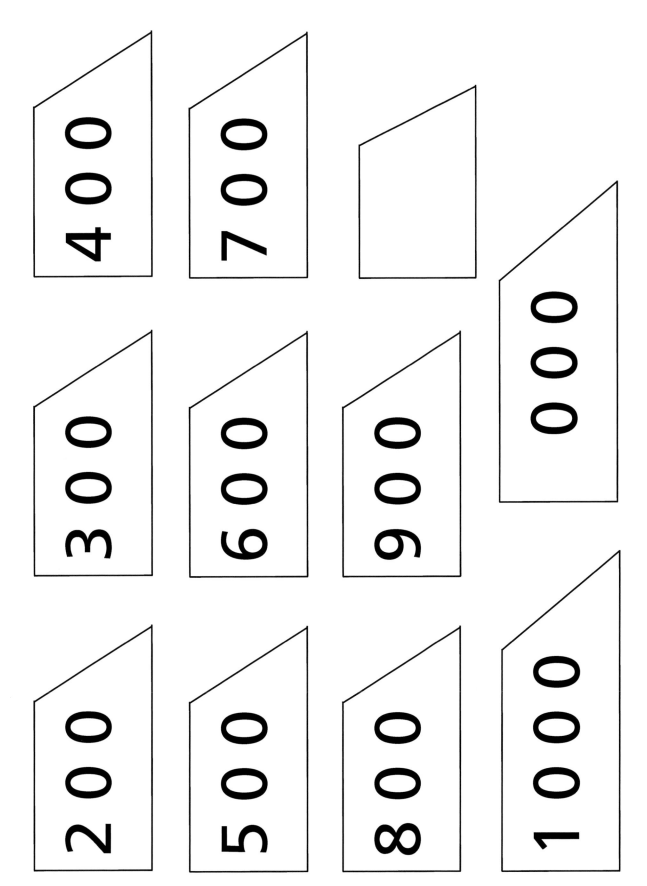

Digit cards

0	1	2	3
4	5	<u>6</u>	7
8	<u>9</u>	0	1
2	3	4	5
<u>6</u>	7	8	<u>9</u>

Digit cards

000	1000	2000	3000
4000	5000	6000	7000
8000	9000	000	1000
2000	3000	4000	5000
6000	7000	8000	9000

Big foot

A game for two to four players

You will need:
- game cards placed in a pack face down on the table
- 'feet' counters or cubes
- number lines with the last number written in

How to play:
- Each of you will need a number line and a pile of 'feet'.
- Take it in turns to pick a card.
- You need to count on from 0 at the beginning of the number line as the card tells you to. So, if the card says 'Count on in 5s to 25', you count from 0 to 25 counting each mark on the number line as a 5.
- Place a foot counter on the mark for 25 and write 25.
- If the card says 'Count on in 2s to 10', you count from 0 to 10 counting each mark as a 2.
- Put a foot counter on the mark for 10 and write 10.
- The aim is to cover all the marks on your line with foot counters.
- The first player to complete their line is the winner, or play so that you score 10 if you are first to complete each line.
- Play several games, using a different colour pencil to write the numbers. Who wins the most?

Count it!

A game for two players

You will need:
- game cards placed in a pack face down on the table beside the game board
- counters – a different colour each
- a pot of money
- a game board

How to play:
- Place your counters on the start rectangle.
- Take it in turns to pick a card from the pack.
- Follow the instructions on your card. So, if the card says 'Start at 0 and count on in 5s to 25', you move your counter around the board five spaces counting 5, 10, 15, 20, 25 in a clockwise direction.
- If the card says 'Start at 40 and count back in 10s to 20', you move in an anti-clockwise direction two spaces counting 30, 20.
- If you land on a 'collect' rectangle, you need to collect and save that amount of money.
- Play continues until your teacher tells you to stop.
- The winner is the player with the most money.

Aliens

A game for two to four players

You will need:
- spinners
- counters
- a game board

How to play:
- You each need a pile of counters.
- Take it in turns to spin the spinner.
- Follow the instructions. For example, if you spin 6 and you are counting in steps of 2, you count 6 steps of 2 (2, 4, 6, 8, 10, 12) then cover the alien marked 12 with a counter.
- If there isn't an alien marked 12 or it is covered, the next person has their go.
- Carry on like this until all the aliens are covered.
- There can be only one counter on an alien, so if your answer is already covered the next player has their turn.
- The winner is the player with the most counters on the board.

Choose your column

A game for two to four players

You will need:
- sets of digit cards from 0 to 9 (in a bag if you prefer)
- a game board
- a spinner

How to play:
- The first player picks two digit cards and makes the highest number they can out of them. Write the number in the grid.
- The second player does the same.
- In the winner column write down who made the highest number.
- Score 10 if you win, 1 if you lose.
- Do this 10 times.
- The winner has the highest score.

Order, Order! – Game 1

A game for two to four players

You will need:
- spinners, dice or digit cards
- a grid sheet to fill in
- pencil

How to play:
- The first player spins the spinner twice and makes the highest number they can out of them.
- They fill in the number in their grid.
- The second player does the same.
- Keep doing this until the grids are full.
- Now have a race to order your numbers from smallest to largest.
- Who won? Score 10.

Order, Order! – Game 2

A game for _____ **players**

Your teacher will tell you what types of numbers you have to make. They might be three-digit numbers, two-digit numbers or whole numbers with 1 decimal place.

You will need:
- spinners, dice or digit cards
- a game sheet to fill in
- pencil

How to play:
- The first player spins _____ times and makes the highest number they can out of these numbers.
- They write the number on their grid.
- The second player does the same.
- Keep doing this until the grid is filled.
- Now have a race to order your numbers from smallest to largest.
- Who won? Score _____

Up, up and away

A game for two to four players

You will need:
- digit cards
- a game board
- pencil and paper

How to play:
- Take it in turns to pick two digit cards and make up two-digit numbers. Write the numbers you make on a piece of paper.
- Keep doing this until you each have 10 numbers. Now it's race time.
- Write the numbers on your game board in order from lowest to highest, putting the lowest number near the ground.
- The winner is the first one to fill the game board in correctly.
- You score 10 points.
- Keep playing. Who can score the most?

Connect

A game for two to four players

You will need:
- dice
- a game board

How to play:
- Throw the dice and total the numbers. If your answer is an odd number cover an O with your counter. If it is an even number cover an E with your counter.
- Take it in turns to do this. You need to try to get four counters in a row, either diagonally, horizontally or vertically. Whoever gets four in a row first, scores 10 points.
- Play again.
- The winner is the player with the highest score at the end of the session.

Star trekking – Game 1

A game for two or three players

You will need:
- dice or digit cards
- a game board

How to play:
- Place your counters on the start.
- Throw the dice and total the numbers. If your answer is an odd number move onto a planet, if it is even move onto a star.
- If your next throw is even when the last throw was odd move your counter sideways onto the star track. Keep going until you reach the end of the track.
- When you get to the end collect a Unifix cube, put it in your space ship and start again with another astronaut.
- The winner is the player with the most Unifix cube crew members at the end of the session.

Star trekking – Game 2

A game for _____ **players**

You will need:
-
-

How to play:
-

-

-

-

-

Round it! – Game 1

A game for two to four players

You will need:
- two sets of digit cards from 0 to 9
- a game board
- ten counters each, a different colour for each player

How to play:
- Take it in turns to pick two digit cards and make a two-digit number.
- Round it to the nearest 10.
- If your new number matches one in a shape, put a counter on it. If not the next player has their turn.
- The winner is the player to cover the most shapes.

Round it! – Game 2

A game for _____ players

You will need:

- _____ sets of digit cards from 0 to 9
- a decimal point each
- a game board
- 10 counters each, a different colour for each player

How to play:
- Take it in turns to pick _____ digit cards and make a _____ number.
- Round it to the nearest _____
- If your new number matches one in a shape, put a counter on it. If not the next player has their turn.
- The winner is the player to cover the most shapes.

Four in a line

A game for two or three players

You will need:
- a pile of digit cards from 1 to 9
- a 0 digit card each
- coloured counters
- a game board

How to play:
- Have some counters and a 0 digit card each.
- Take it in turns to pick 2 digit cards and put them beside your 0 card to make a 3-digit number; for example, if you pick 4 and 6, put them beside your 0 to make 460 or 640.
- Look on the game board to find a number that can be rounded to it, for example 643. Place a counter on the number.
- Now it's the next person's turn.
- If there is no number available the next player takes their turn.
- Carry on playing until one of you gets 4 counters in a row, either horizontally, vertically or diagonally.

Climb the ladder

A game for two to four players

You will need:
- number cards
- a game board
- pencil

How to play:
- The aim is to fill the ladder with 10 two-digit numbers in order from lowest at the bottom to highest at the top.
- Take it in turn to pick a number.
- All of you, individually, decide where to put the number on your ladder and put it in the appropriate space.
- If there is no space put it on the fire truck.
- The winner is the first player with a completed ladder and the fewest numbers on the truck.
- You score 10 points.
- Play the game as many times as possible during the session.
- The overall winner is the child with the most points.

Elephant estimating

A game for two to six players

You will need:
- a game board
- lots of cubes/counters
- paper and pencil

How to play:
- One player takes a handful (or more) of cubes and drops them on the table.
- Everyone now has to immediately estimate how many cubes there are – no counting, anyone who counts is disqualified from that round!
- Write your estimates on paper and show each other.
- Now count the cubes.
- The player (or players) with the closest estimate wins a counter to put on their elephant game board.
- The winner is the player with the most counters on their elephant at the end of the session.

The approximation game

A game for two to four players

You will need:
- calculation cards
- a game board
- 1 different coloured counter each
- pencil and paper, number line (calculator if your teacher allows it)

How to play:
- Take it in turns to pick a calculation card. Estimate the answer by rounding to the nearest ten.
- Explain to your group how you got your estimation.
- Ask the other players to find the real answer on a calculator.
- Find the difference between your estimate and the real answer.
- Move on that number of stepping stones. The winner is the player who reaches home last, because their approximations will have been the closest to the real answers.

Bingo

A game for the whole class or two to four players

You will need:
- a bingo card
- pencil
- a caller with a list of questions

How to play:
- The caller reads out the questions.
- Players cross out numbers that fit the question.
- When a whole card is crossed out shout 'Bingo'.
- The caller must check the card!

A game for _____ players

You will need:
-
-
-

How to play:
-